POSTCARDS from TIMES SQUARE

George J. Lankevich

SQUAREONE PUBLISHERS

Cover Design: Phaedra Mastrocola
In-House Editing: Joanne Abrams
Interior Design: Phaedra Mastrocola
Typesetting: Gary A. Rosenberg
Printing: Paragon Press, Honesdale, PA

Square One Publishers | Garden City Park, NY 11040 | **516-535-2010** | www.squareonepublishers.com

Library of Congress Cataloging-in-Publication Data

Lankevich, George J., 1939–
Postcards from Times Square : sights & sentiments from the last century / George J. Lankevich.
p. cm.
Includes index.
ISBN 0-7570-0100-9 (quality pbk.)
1. Times Square (New York, N.Y.)—History. 2. New York (N.Y.)—History—1898-1951. 3. New York (N.Y.)—History—1951- 4. Times Square (New York, N.Y.)—History—Pictorial works. 5. New York (N.Y.)—History—Pictorial works. 6. Postcards—New York (State)—New York. I. Title.
F128.65.T5 L36 2001
974.7'1—dc21

2001000187

Printed in the United States of America

10 9 8 7 6 5 4 3 2 1

Contents

Introduction, 1

Chapter One

Act One, 1904–1919 7

The New York to Paris Auto Race 16

Adolph Ochs and the *Times* Tower 19

The Theater District 27

The Eastern Edge 44

The Grand Hotels of Times Square 48

The Restaurants of Times Square 51

Chapter Two

Between the Wars, 1919–1941 63

The Great Ziegfeld 67

The Paramount 69

Commercialism and the Great White Way 71

Rockefeller Center 75

Radio City Music Hall 76

Roseland 80

Vaudeville and Burlesque on Broadway 87

Chapter Three

From Triumph to Twilight, 1941–1975 97

Miss Liberty 103

Times Square Goes to War 105

Palaces on Times Square 117

The Palace 123

Times Square in Decline 147

The Allied Chemical Tower 153

Chapter Four

Resurrection, 1975–2000 155

Rebuilding Times Square 161

The Saga of the Empire Theater 165

Conclusion 167

Index 169

Acknowledgments

The publisher and author have made every attempt to contact all existing copyright holders. We would like to thank the many postcard dealers and collectors who helped make this book possible. We are especially grateful to the people and organizations who allowed us to use the following postcards:

- The postcards on pages 5, 34, 36, 52, 53, 55, 68, 83, 85, 86, 109, 123, and 124 were reprinted courtesy of the Bob Stonehill Archive.
- The postcards on pages 65 and 135 were reprinted courtesy of Mark E. Schwartz.
- The postcards on pages 1, 3, 4, 120, 129, 147, 148, 151, 152, and 157 were reprinted courtesy of Seymour B. Durst Old York Library at the Graduate Center of the City University of New York.
- The postcard on page 35 (right) was reprinted courtesy of the Shubert Archive.
- The postcard on page 146 (right) was reprinted courtesy of Karen Minutoli.
- The postcard on page 168 and several photos of today's Times Square were reprinted courtesy of Selwyn Cooper.
- The postcards on pages 21, 137, 141 (right), and 153 were reprinted courtesy of the Tony Gulizia Collection.
- The postcards on pages 16, 17 (left), 103, 104, 119, 127, and 128 were reprinted courtesy of Todd Harvey.
- The postcards on pages 158, 159, and 160 were reproduced by permission of Alfred Mainzer, Inc.
- We would also like to acknowledge the help of Bunny Moses of Bell, Book & Candle.

The Casino Theater at 39th Street and Broadway—*Detail*

INTRODUCTION
Crossroads of the World

New York City is a world metropolis offering the widest variety of experiences to residents, to the commuters who daily fill its streets, and especially to the 38 million-plus visitors who annually arrive to sample its wonders. The contemporary bustling city is filled with places that absolutely *must* be seen—Miss Liberty in the harbor; internationally famed skyscrapers; and urban neighborhoods as varied as Little Italy, Chinatown, and Harlem. Every American "knows" such places through movies, but nothing matches the thrill of personal experience. As early as 1902, *Harper's Weekly* asserted there was "no American so lowly in condition, or so remote geographically, but cherishes in his heart the ambition to see New York at least once before he dies." The magazine was correct then, and its judgment remains true today. And for an entire century, tourists have considered a trip to Manhattan incomplete unless they could stand in and marvel at Times Square. Famous around the globe, the intersection of 42nd Street and Broadway is universally considered the beating heart of the Big Apple, its entertainment center, the "Crossroads of the World." Everyone believes that if you stand at that fabled site, you will soon meet somebody from your home town. Perhaps no other place on earth is so attractive, so familiar, and so dangerously forbidding—all at the same time.

Postcards from Times Square traces the history of a world-renowned landmark across a tumultuous century, documents its changing face, and examines its enduring mystique. Like the larger metropolis it symbolizes, Times Square has undergone dramatic changes over time, yet it maintains its undeniable allure for both tourists and natives. Perhaps the area's unique ability to reshape itself every generation is the reason it continues to draw visitors from across the world; it is always the same, yet different. It is hard to tire of Times Square, whether you are seeing it for the first time or you pass through it every day on your way to work. It is the one part of the world's greatest city that has become transcendent, leaping across all cultural barriers to become an international entertainment center. Times Square is theater, movies, bright lights, fine dining, nightclubs, elegance, and more than a hint of threat. Everything about it seems outsized yet familiar, inspiring both a sense of awe and a shiver of recognition. By tracing its many incarnations, we are introduced to the even greater miracle of New York City.

Most people know that "old New York was once New Amsterdam," a Dutch trading settlement established around the Battery (southern Manhattan Island) early in the seventeenth century. But relatively few appreciate how slowly the physical city expanded as it became America's metropolis. Early in the nineteenth century, John Jacob Astor, a land speculator with great faith in New York's future, decided to accumulate large tracts of land in still undeveloped midtown Manhattan. Although Astor ruefully lamented his inability "to buy every foot of land on the island," he purchased as much as his fortune allowed. In 1811, city planners optimistically established a street map of the entire island that designated a yet unbuilt 42nd Street as a major east-west artery. Among the many pieces of cheap mid-island land Astor acquired was the farm of John Norton, which extended from future 42nd Street to 46th Street, and from Broadway over to the Hudson River. The property included the Great Kill stream, which meandered westward along what would later become 42nd Street, and passed a small village before emptying into the river. When Astor bought the farmland, it held far more animals than people; well into the 1830s, 42nd Street remained little more than a cow path along which cattle were driven from landing sites on the Hudson River to slaughterhouses on the east side of Manhattan. But land values continued to increase, and at his death in 1848, Astor was the richest man in the United States. His son, William Backhouse Astor, "the landlord of New York," anticipated the housing needs of a growing city, and began to fill the once rural district with rows of brownstone houses available for rent or purchase.

When the Civil War began in 1861, New York held 800,000 people, but the city proper was still centered below 14th Street. The area around Broadway in the 40s was far from fully settled, but growing numbers of neighborhood workers found employment in the farms of northern Manhattan or in the construction of Central Park. Wartime prosperity and a constantly rising city population stimulated further development, and by 1870, the area had become a center for the carriage, wagon, and harness trades. Another step towards prominence came in 1881, when William K. Vanderbilt and several of his gentlemen friends—needing a decent place to trade horses, stable their thoroughbreds, and practice riding—financed construction of the American Horse Exchange at 50th Street. Their building remains in Times Square today, disguised as the Winter Garden Theater. Although their surroundings were definitely working class, the horsemen reveled in the city's designation of the area as Longacre Square, after the

NO. 305. E. REACH, TORONTO

THE "CASINO." A CONCERT HALL WITH ROOF GARDEN

The Casino Theater

carriage district of London. They understood that the term "square" was not geometrically accurate—Longacre was really two triangles formed by the intersection of major north-south roads—but the name added a bit of class to the neighborhood. None suspected that within thirty years, their playground would become New York's primary theater district and enjoy international fame.

In the last decades of the nineteenth century, the relentless northward movement of New York and the enormous demands of its population for work, news, and entertainment, led to the creation of a new center of city life. Until the 1870s, "Newspaper Row" clustered around the City Hall-Brooklyn Bridge area, but then the metropolitan journals began to join the northern tide. In 1875, for example, the *Tribune* hired America's leading architect Richard Morris Hunt to design its new building near 34th Street. Competition for circulation and influence was the essence of the newspaper business for the rest of the century, but no newspaper dared to venture as far north as 42nd Street. If a single factor can be called vital in the emergence of Times Square as a city center, it was the 1902 decision of the *The New York Times* to place its headquarters there.

Like the clannish newspapers, Manhattan's entertainment district had also clustered in a relatively small area between Union Square and Madison Square. But in the 1880s, a line of theaters began to move north along the spine of Broadway. It was then that people first remarked on a "White Way" of gas lights that visibly drew audiences out of Madison Square. Theaters like the Fifth Avenue, The Strand, The Garrick, and Weber and Fields' Music Hall gradually extended the theater district northward, moving from 23rd Street into the mid-30s. It appeared that the edge of culture and civilization was on the march—although as late as 1899, when Manhattan boasted a total of twenty-two theaters, only one of them was in Longacre Square. Perhaps the boldest move occurred in October 1882, when the 1,300-seat Casino Theater, whose specialty was comic opera, opened for business on Broadway at 39th Street. The Casino consistently attracted large nighttime audiences to its Moorish auditorium, and became a "must see" location when it introduced the Florodora girls to New York in 1900. Even more important in drawing an upscale audience to the emerging theater district was the new 3,700-seat Metropolitan Opera House, which opened in 1883 with a performance of *Faust*. Neither the Casino nor the Met survives today, but in the last years of the nineteenth century, these two buildings at Broadway and 39th Street provided definite proof that the entertainment center for both middle class and highbrow culture had shifted northward.

In 1898, Greater New York was created when Manhattan was joined with surrounding areas to become a single city. A final vital factor in the creation of Times Square was the development of a mass transportation system for a metropolis that suddenly had a population of 3.4 million people spread over five boroughs. Greater New York would build a subway, and when it opened in 1904, one of its planned stops would be in the Longacre Square area. But until the subway proved itself, existing elevated lines—commonly called *els*—running north would remain essential, and had to be improved. In 1905, city planners extended the Sixth Avenue Elevated Line westward along 53rd Street to link up with the Ninth Avenue Elevated. Like the Gaity Theater and the Metropolitan Opera House to the south, the elevated structure established a boundary for the entertainment district that was to emerge in Times Square. In addition to the subway and the els, the creation of major railroad terminals at Penn Station (1911) and Grand Central (1913) provided the means for thousands of people to take pleasure trips into the area. One of the first businesses to recognize the changing reality was the Pabst Brewery, whose directors opened a hotel at the southern edge of the Longacre in 1899, anticipating a growing demand for rooms. Significantly, the Pabst Hotel's main entrance faced southward towards the Casino and the Met. During the next twenty years, Times Square would take shape in the blocks between the elevated tracks and the edge of the theater district.

Florodora Girls–*Detail*

Opened by a beer manufacturer, the Pabst Hotel showed that the business community had faith in the future of the area. [c. 1900]

Only in retrospect is it possible to identify the various forces that made Times Square come to life. Visitors to the metropolis rightly see the entertainment district not as a subject for historical study, but rather as a place of fun and excitement, an experience they wish to remember forever. For generations, the preferred way to preserve those memories was not by reading dry history books, but by purchasing picture postcards that recalled the amazing sights they had witnessed. And is there a better way for tourists to "keep in touch" with loved ones—to prove that they have braved the dangers, delights, and decadence of Times Square—than by sending a postcard home?

Practically everyone has mailed a postcard at some time in his or her life. Many Americans remember that Benjamin Franklin organized the first postal system, and stamp collectors know that the first United States postage stamps appeared in 1847. But it may come as a bit of a shock to learn that the postcard is a relative newcomer to American life. During the 1860s, a few privately printed cards made their way through the United States mails, largely as advertisements, but not until May 13, 1873 did the government first issue postal cards. Costing only a penny, these unillustrated cards provided Washington with a monopoly over the sending of reduced-rate messages for the next twenty years. During that time, a few souvenir cards with a picture or a message on one side were delivered, but only at the 2-cent letter rate. Not until Chicago's 1893 Colombian Exposition did the United States Post Office authorize the issuance of picture postcards, awarding Charles Goldsmith a franchise to produce sets of designs printed on government penny cards. Selling at ten for 25 cents, and later twelve for 25 cents, these were the forerunners of privately printed cards. The great success of the Colombian Exposition cards, and their desirability as collectibles, led some entrepreneurs to offer their own souvenir cards. But if these held any written message, they could be delivered only if the standard 2-cent letter rate was paid. Only when forwarded as printed matter—without any added message—did the cards cost a penny to send. Americans who wished to send a penny message to family and friends had to purchase the government card.

The outcry against such inequality led Congress to pass the Private Mailing Act of May 19, 1898. Manufacturers were permitted to offer Private Mailing Cards (PMCs) or Souvenir Cards, which could be mailed for the same penny as a government card. Mostly printed in Germany or Austria-Hungary, the PMCs were beautifully produced, but their message space was limited to a small portion on the front of the card, beneath or next to the picture. The postal service permitted the back to contain only an address. Because of their foreign origin, some of these lovely early cards contained errors in identification and printing, yet by 1905, over a billion were being sold annually. Collecting them was a hobby enjoyed by many.

The modern postcard was created on March 1, 1907, when postal authorities decided that a "split back," offering half the back side for a message and the other for an address, was acceptable. A rollback of federal policy had been effected, and the collection of penny postcards escalated into a national mania. The American Souvenir Card Company offered sets of fifteen cities, and when New York hosted the Hudson-Fulton Celebration in 1909, postcards were sold everywhere. Significantly, the first patent for a wire rack holding cards was issued in 1908, and in 1911, vending machines for cards were introduced to prevent consumer theft from open racks. Only the outbreak of World War I, and the gradual halt of imports from the Central Powers, ended the postcard craze.

Deltiology is the collection and study of postcards, and today it remains the hobby of choice for millions. By 1917, the postcard was an accepted part of American life, but domestically produced cards were of inferior quality, and often reproduced past images. Moreover, in order to save ink and reduce costs, most domestic cards from 1917 to 1930 had a narrow white border around the image. During the Great Depression, improved technology and higher rag-content stock led to "linen" textured postcards. After 1945, the "chrome" finished cards familiar today were produced domestically. But as costs escalated and years passed, printers found other sources of revenue. Most contemporary postcards are manufactured overseas.

But whatever its format or origin, there is little doubt that the postcard transcends its form. It offers a glimpse of the unfamiliar, the sight of a place worth visiting and remembering, a familiar voice that might otherwise not be heard. Postcards are quickly sent, cost less than a letter to mail, and convey greetings from someone on the move. Those who receive them have a memento, an inducement to travel, a pledge of affection. No city has been better represented in postcards than New York, the national metropolis, and because Times Square became a destination for most travelers, we have a unique record of its development. In the following pages, the images of Times Square and the reaction of its visitors provide insights into its history. More than five generations of tourists have visited Times Square, experienced its atmosphere, been attracted or repelled by its gaudiness, and lived to tell the tale. Enter the boundaries of America's common crossroads, and enjoy a trip through time.

CHAPTER ONE

Act One, 1904–1919

On January 1, 1898, the dream of expanding New York City and consolidating Manhattan with Brooklyn, the Bronx, Queens, and Staten Island was realized. Greater New York—boasting a population of 3.4 million, and a fifteen-fold increase in land size—had emerged fully grown, and its future prosperity appeared to be limitless. Development was the watchword of the era, and Manhattan's enterprising businessmen moved quickly to seek commercial advantage in the altered environment. Many believed that Longacre Square was the next area the ever-shifting Manhattan population would engulf, so brownstone apartments, hotels, and restaurants quickly appeared to fill their needs.

Broadway, New York

Oscar Hammerstein I had anticipated change, and in 1895, he became the first theatrical entrepreneur to cross the northern boundary of the "Rialto"—New York's theater district. Hammerstein opened the Olympia theater complex in the square at 45th Street. Unsuccessful there, he would soon build the Victoria on 42nd Street. His audacity was soon matched by the publisher of *The New York Times*. In 1902, Adolph Ochs purchased the lease of the Pabst Hotel, ordered its demolition, and made plans to build a new home for his newspaper. Ochs knew that New York was building a subway that would pass through the area, and intended to make his headquarters the centerpiece of the new neighborhood. Times Square was formally named on April 19, 1904, when city aldermen followed the recommendation of Mayor George McClellan, and changed the name of Longacre Square. From the start of its history, an emphasis on both entertainment and news characterized Times Square.

Stimulated by Hammerstein's example, the first decade of the new century saw a surge of theater construction in and around Times Square. From 1903 to 1907, nine new showplaces were opened on 42nd Street, and it became the unquestioned center of Manhattan's theatrical activity. By 1920, New York City had a total of fifty theaters, and most of them were located in the Times Square area.

But theatrical performances were only part of Times Square's attraction. No area of the city offered a more imposing choice of restaurants. With both legitimate theater and vaudeville audiences flocking to Times Square, eating places of every variety soon dotted the flourishing district. Oyster bars, beer gardens, and lobster houses quickly opened, but Rector's, established in 1899, led the way in fine dining. At the cost of half a million dollars, Charles and George Rector "brought Paris to New York" in their restaurant on Broadway, across from the *Times* Tower. Financier "Diamond Jim" Brady, often accompanied by entertainer Lillian Russell, boasted that he alone was Rector's "twenty-five best customers," and for twenty years, the establishment set the standard for *haute cuisine*. But competition was fierce, and rivals such as Shanley's on 43rd Street, Churchill's on 48th Street, and Murray's Roman Gardens on 42nd Street, each had their devotees. Diners preferring more conventional, less adventurous surroundings spent their money at Delmonico's or Sherry's on Fifth Avenue, fully two blocks from the bright lights of Broadway. The heyday of such glamorous dining ended with Prohibition, when legitimate establishments found it impossible to compete with those that illegally served liquor.

Finally, there was the unique thrill of seeing Times Square lit up in splendor. As early as 1901, O.J. Gude, one of America's first advertising geniuses, decided that Times Square was the perfect environment for his craft. For the next two decades, Gude did his very best to turn the area into an incandescent dreamland. Marvelous arrays of bulbs offering products unfamiliar to modern consumers drew the eyes of the million people who daily passed through the area. And the signs of the movie palace attractions added even more illumination. Not even the shock of World War I could extinguish the white lights of Times Square, and in the 1920s, neon would make them even more colorful. Sadly, it is also true that the brightness of 42nd Street and Broadway was surrounded by "red light" establishments, a reminder that entertainment has a very broad definition.

By 1920, the nature of the Times Square district was well established. It was an area where theater flourished, movies played, gourmets dined, and commercialism reigned. It was home to the Yacht Club and the Lamb's Club, vaudeville and drama, the finest hotels and the rankest "bawdy house." It was an entertainment center that could fulfill every desire. What is perhaps most surprising is that it would retain that reputation for the rest of the century.

Longacre Square officially became Times Square in April 1904. The *Times* Tower was flanked by the Olympia complex (left) and the Astor Hotel (right). Note the informal traffic pattern. [c.1906]

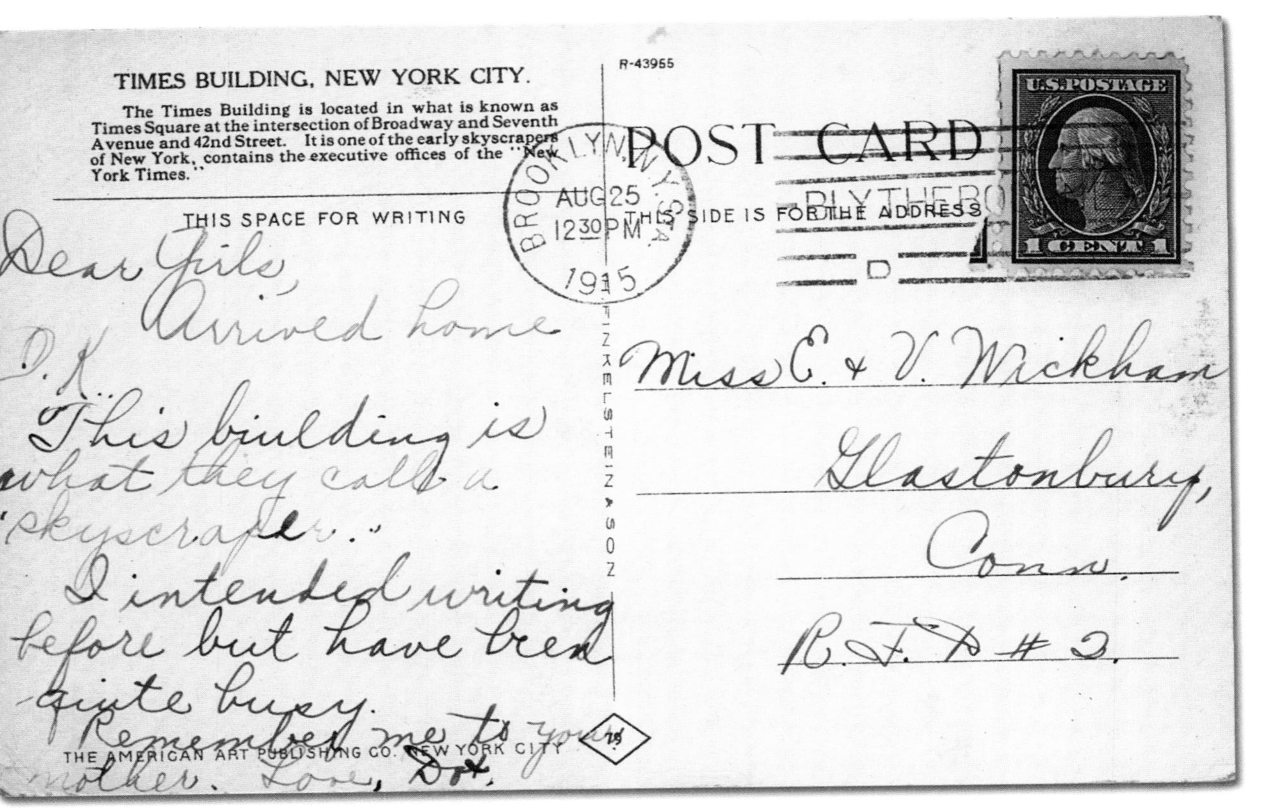
TIMES BUILDING, NEW YORK CITY.

The Times Building is located in what is known as Times Square at the intersection of Broadway and Seventh Avenue and 42nd Street. It is one of the early skyscrapers of New York, contains the executive offices of the "New York Times."

THIS SPACE FOR WRITING

Dear Girls,
Arrived home O.K.
This building is what they call a "skyscraper."
I intended writing before but have been quite busy.
Remember me to your mother. Love, Dot.

R-43955

POST CARD

THIS SIDE IS FOR THE ADDRESS

Miss E. & V. Wickham
Glastonbury,
Conn.
R.F.D # 2.

H. FINKELSTEIN & SON

THE AMERICAN ART PUBLISHING CO. NEW YORK CITY

By 1907, Times Square meant entertainment and excitement. Walkers approaching from the south on Broadway saw Ochs' tower as their goal. [c.1907]

The Met, its splendid interior encased in ordinary yellow brick, was part of the Times Square mystique. From 1904 to 1919, Enrico Caruso sang at each opening night. [c.1905]

Five million passengers used the Times Square subway station from 1904 to 1905, making it the most popular local stop in the system. Note the different kiosk designs. [c.1906]

During its first year, the subway system carried 106 million passengers at a nickel each—a bargain fare that, until July 1, 1947, was enjoyed by New Yorkers and tourists alike. [c.1906]

The triangles created by the intersection of Broadway and Seventh Avenue are apparent in this postcard, which also implies the rivalry between the hotels Knickerbocker (left) and Astor (right). [c.1908]

The New York to Paris Auto Race

The year 1908 was an important one for America's automobile industry. Buick was the year's single leading manufacturer, with 8,487 cars; William Durant was organizing General Motors; Henry Ford made waves when he introduced his Model T, "the motorcar for the great multitudes." And Times Square launched the greatest car race in history, a 21,000-mile trip across three continents from New York to Paris. Six racing teams revved up their engines before the Astor Hotel in February 1908 to begin an unprecedented attack on a world without roads. On July 30, the German entry arrived in Paris, followed four days later by the American team in their Thomas Flyer. But when the judges learned that the Germans had transported their car by train for part of the race, they awarded first prize to the stalwart Americans.

An estimated quarter million New Yorkers cheered as six cars raced north towards 110th Street, the first leg of their marathon race. [c.1908]

Ever-changing "spectacular" signs marked the passage into Times Square by day and night. Even in 1911, pedestrians and traffic maneuvered for street space. [c.1911]

POST CARD

TIMES SQ. STA. N.Y. MAR 6 3-PM 1913

U.S. POSTAGE

THIS SPACE MAY BE USED FOR WRITING

THIS SIDE FOR THE ADDRESS ONLY

I saw the moving pictures of the inauguration this a.m. here. They were fine, you could see better than if you were in Washington. These machines were set up in choise places.

Very truly
Chester.

Miss Mabel Trumbauer.
Quakertown,
Penna.

Success Postal Card Co., Pub., New York, No. 1059

Adolph Ochs and the *Times* Tower

The New York Times was one of many city newspapers that made its headquarters on Park Row in lower Manhattan. Founded in 1851, the *Times* had rarely been the most read newspaper in the city. During the 1870s, it played a leading role in overthrowing the Tweed Ring by publishing exposés that led to the indictment and conviction of America's most infamous political "boss." But despite such coups, the paper was not popular with the masses, and entered receivership in the 1890s. Adolph Ochs (1853–1935) purchased the failing journal in 1896 for a mere $75,000, and quickly restored its prestige by providing impartial news "without fear or favor." Ochs' paper offered a sober, increasingly valued alternative to the "yellow journalism" characteristic of the decade, and on February 10, 1897, he added to his front page a pledge to provide "All the News That's Fit to Print."

The ambitious Ochs was well aware that the rival *New York Herald* had left "Newspaper Row" in the 1870s, and that Herald Square had been named to honor its presence on 34th Street. In 1902, Ochs decided that the *Times* would move north to Longacre Square, and occupy a new building on the site of the Pabst Hotel at the intersection of 42nd Street, Broadway, and Seventh Avenue. Designed by Cyrus Eidlitz in Italian Renaissance style, the new *Times* Tower would be a twenty-five-story (362-foot) structure of terra cotta and pink granite, and rank as the second tallest building in Manhattan. Looking north over Longacre Square, it would totally dominate an area where no other building surpassed six stories.

Ochs believed that his leap from "Newspaper Row" to 42nd Street would make the *Times* the focus of a New York public square—a civic center for a new century that would reflect the values and elegance of his paper. He had an expansive view of the city's future, and when his daughter, Iphigenia, set the cornerstone on January 18, 1904, the paper's main entrance faced east towards the rising sun and midtown business. Ochs also put his presses into the "deepest hole in New York," placing them below the municipal subway line then under construction into Longacre Square. With the support of August Belmont, who was financing the subway, Ochs convinced Mayor George McClellan to rename the district. On April 19, 1904, the rising newspaper headquarters became the centerpiece of "Times Square." On December 31, over 200,000 New Yorkers filled the streets around the tower to watch a fireworks display, beginning a celebratory tradition that is now shared by the entire world. Before Ochs' first holiday party, city residents who wished to greet the New Year had gathered at Wall Street to hear the chimes of Trinity Church.

Fireworks remained the main entertainment in Times Square for the next three years, but on December 31, 1908, the New Year was heralded by the dropping of an illuminated ball atop the tower. Although this first ball fell less than a meter in twenty seconds, the *Times* had created a New York moment that would be halted only by dim-out regulations during World War II. When Allied victory seemed assured in December 1944, the ceremonial drop was resumed. It is interesting to note that the ball itself, which in prewar days had weighed some 600 pounds, was lighter by two-thirds because of improvements in wartime metallurgy. For a long

The Florentine-style *Times* Tower dominated the entry to Times Square, and until 1926, was unrivaled in height. [c.1912]

Adolph Ochs an

time, employees of the Artkraft Corporation were in charge of the proceedings, and these volunteers performed with military precision. For several years in the 1980s, a "Big (red) Apple" was dropped instead of the glowing white ball, but the original tradition was then resumed. On December 31, 1999, over a billion people watched as a Waterford crystal ball descended a seventy-seven-foot pole to greet what was considered to be the new millennium. Such global reach fulfilled the highest hopes of Ochs when he built a new home for his newspaper.

But even in 1905, it was apparent that Ochs' gamble had succeeded. Over 5 million New Yorkers used the Times Square subway stop in 1904 and 1905, and after the great "H" of the IRT system was completed in 1913, Times Square ranked as New York's busiest station. But as the *Times* became the "newspaper of record," it rapidly outgrew the tiny floor space of the tower, and in 1913, had to transfer operations to 229 West 43rd Street. Nevertheless, the paper retained advertising operations on 42nd Street, and continued to post news items, including fight and baseball results, on bulletin boards at the base of its building. The Hotelings kiosk, carrying dozens of out-of-town newspapers, opened at the north end of the tower in 1912. Electric signs announcing the latest news flashes were introduced in 1910, but the famous Motogram "zipper" around the tower did not operate until 1928. Although the structure was sold in 1961, and has gone through incarnations as the Allied Chemical Tower and One Times Square, in popular memory it remains the *Times* Tower. Now used primarily as a billboard, the tower has been the most prominent image of Times Square for over half a century.

O.J. Gude, pioneer of modern advertising, was responsible for transforming Times Square into the heart of the "Great White Way." 1905 was the first year that "Miss Heatherbloom" billowed and glowed. [c.1910]

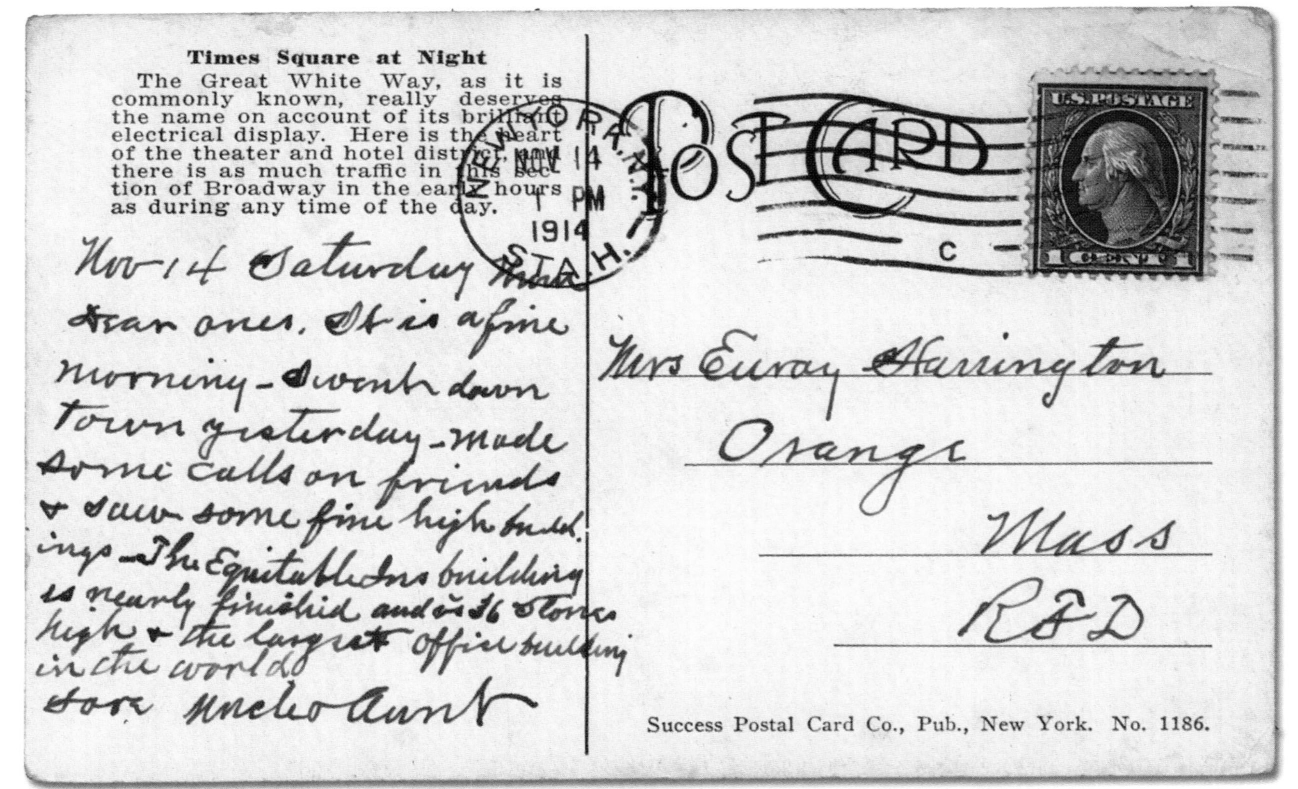
Times Square at Night
The Great White Way, as it is commonly known, really deserves the name on account of its brilliant electrical display. Here is the heart of the theater and hotel district, and there is as much traffic in this section of Broadway in the early hours as during any time of the day.
NEW YORK, N.Y. NOV 14 1 PM 1914 STA. H.
POST CARD
U.S. POSTAGE
1 CENT 1
C
Nov 14 Saturday
Dear ones. It is a fine
morning - I went down
town yesterday - made
some calls on friends
& saw some fine high build-
ings - The Equitable Ins building
is nearly finished and is 36 stories
high & the largest office building
in the world
Love Uncle & Aunt
Mrs Euray Harrington
Orange
Mass
RFD
Success Postal Card Co., Pub., New York. No. 1186.

Times Square appears almost sedate in this postcard. The north tower, here almost bare, would soon become the most prized advertising space in Manhattan. [c.1912]

The huge success of the Astor fostered Manhattan's first hotel building boom. By 1919, the Plaza, Vanderbilt, Biltmore, Commodore, McAlpin, Pennsylvania, and Ritz Carlton had followed. [c.1905]

Tourists and Times Square have always gone together. This vintage coach would surely be filled to overflowing today. [c.1905]

Totally illuminated by electricity, Oscar Hammerstein's Olympia complex changed a workingman's district into an entertainment center. Hammerstein lost control of the complex by 1898, and the Olympia was subdivided. [c.1905]

The Theater District

New York City, always a shipping port visited annually by thousands of sailors from a score of nations, has throughout its long history never lacked for saloons and brothels. But creating entertainment for the middle and upper classes became more important as the city moved beyond its early crudeness and attained ever-increasing prominence in the new nation. By the mid-nineteenth century, Manhattan had seized America's intellectual leadership in publishing, music, and theater—a position that it retains today—and municipal elites could enjoy the wide variety of cultural pursuits for which the city became famed. Within the maturing metropolis, the focal point for such activities was constantly moving as it attempted to keep a modest distance between the well-to-do and the rabble. Thus, as the city grew, the legitimate theater migrated northward, away from the crowded streets of the immigrant sections and into areas more convenient for the monied classes.

Originally located in the City Hall area, the theater district of New York gradually migrated uptown to 14th Street and Union Square, and subsequently, as the nineteenth century progressed, to Madison and Herald Squares. By the 1890s, theater canopies were a vital part of the "White Way" of lights traveling north along the spine of Broadway from 23rd to 40th Streets. Indicative of the northward shift was the famous battle between the established patrons of the Academy of Music on 14th Street and the *nouveau riche,* who constructed a rival Metropolitan Opera on 39th Street in 1883. Buttressed by the presence of the Casino Theater (1882) and Charles Frohman's Empire (1893), the theater district seemed poised for yet another northward migration.

The key figure in bringing theater to the "dismal reaches" above 42nd Street—a rough and tumble "thieves lair" feared by good citizens—was Oscar Hammerstein I. A mighty dynamo at five feet four inches, Hammerstein had already made and lost several fortunes when he turned his attention to the Longacre. Using settlement money gained from suing his partners in a 34th Street theater operation, Hammerstein ordered construction of a theatrical complex to fill the entire block on east Broadway, between 44th and 45th Streets. Designed by J.B. McElfratich, the Olympia was dominated by the Lyric Theater, where eleven tiers containing 124 boxes surrounded the stage. Hammerstein intended to present dramatic fare at the Lyric, but the Olympia also featured a Music Hall, a Concert Hall, and a glass-enclosed roof-garden/cabaret, as well as cafés, a promenade, billiards, baths, and a bowling alley. In November 1895, Hammerstein, a genius in public relations before the craft was even invented, arranged to print 4,000 extra tickets for opening night ceremonies, guaranteeing both a riot and additional press coverage. But even with prices set at the then-astronomic levels of 50 cents to $1.50, the Olympia could not cover costs, and Hammerstein lost control of his operation by 1898. The various parts of the Olympia continued as the New York and Criterion Theaters, as well as the *Jardin de Danse* roof complex.

But the irrepressible Hammerstein was already planning new ventures, and in 1899, he opened the Victoria Theater on the corner of Seventh Avenue and 42nd Street. During the first decade of the new century, nine new theaters rapidly filled

The Theater District

the block between Seventh Avenue and T. Henry French's American Theater, located on Eighth Avenue. The Republic, another Lyric, the Liberty, and the Apollo rapidly appeared to help create the legend of 42nd Street. Other new Manhattan stages included the Lyceum Theater (1903), whose elegant façade may still be viewed on West 45th Street; the Hippodrome (1906), the world's largest theater with 5,500 seats; and the Winter Garden, which was created from Vanderbilt's American Horse Exchange (1911). But among all its many rivals in the Times Square area, the Victoria was surpassed only by the New Amsterdam, the "House Beautiful" constructed in 1903 by Herts and Tallent at twice the cost of an average playhouse. Planned as the prime stage for the Klaw/Erlanger Theater Syndicate established in 1896, the New Amsterdam featured a roof garden as extensive as that of Hammerstein's "paradise" atop the Victoria, as well as the first cantilevered balcony in the metropolis. The New Amsterdam hosted the *Ziegfeld Follies* from 1913 to 1927, and its elegant interior has been recently restored by the Disney Company. Because of its importance to the Syndicate, the New Amsterdam always obtained the best dramatic shows, and the Victoria soon specialized in offering the finest vaudeville shows in the city.

By 1910, Manhattan had over thirty houses, and by 1920, the total had soared to fifty, with most of them located in the Times Square district. People attended the theater more often in these decades, and demanded constantly changing attractions, so there was always work for singers, dancers, and actors. Even extravaganzas like the *Ziegfeld Follies* did not aspire to a long run. Unlike the long-running shows of the present day, variety and change was the rule on the Great White Way of the early century. For example, in 1915—a year of limited expectations due to world war in Europe—a total of 133 new productions were presented in forty-two theaters.

Times Square was not to be the staid civic center devoutly sought by Adolph Ochs. Rather, it became an entertainment mecca, fulfilling the vision of Oscar Hammerstein. In less than a decade, the heart of the theater district had moved uptown and discovered its permanent location for the next century.

Until World War I, "Broadway Battleships" were the primary street transport in Times Square. [c.1912]

Under the management of Willie Hammerstein, the ▶ Victoria offered exceptional vaudeville. Its roof garden held a "Swiss farm" with a water wheel to beguile post-theater crowds. [c.1912]

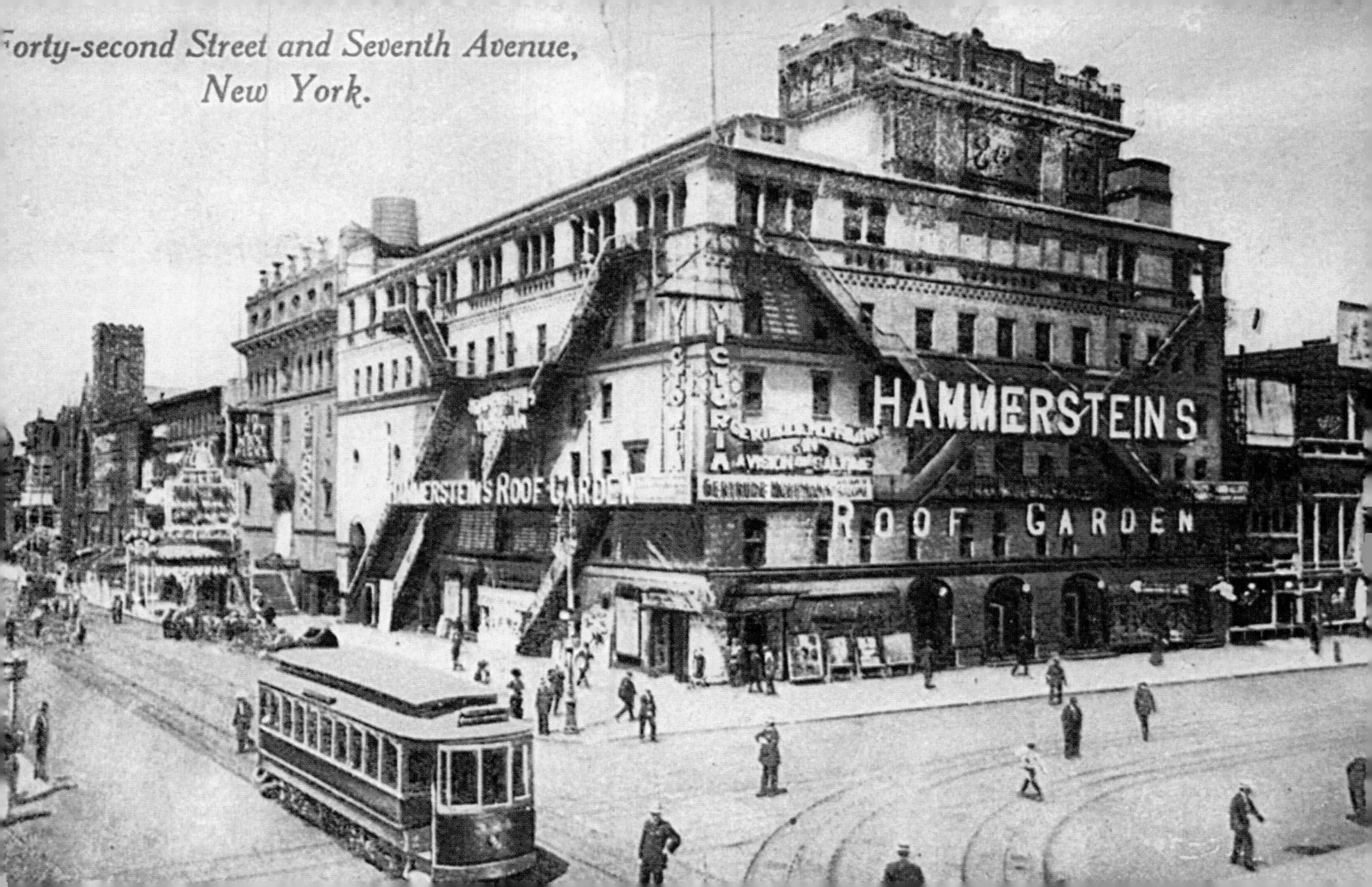
Forty-second Street and Seventh Avenue,
New York.
VICTORIA
HAMMERSTEIN'S ROOF GARDEN
HAMMERSTEINS
ROOF GARDEN

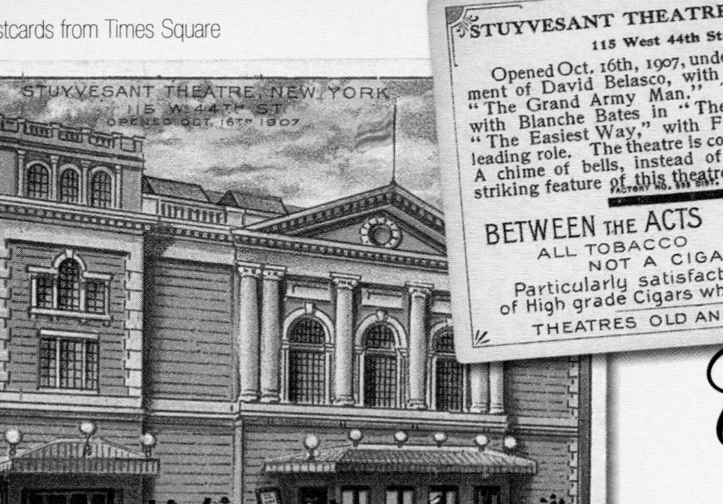

STUYVESANT THEATRE, NEW YORK
115 West 44th Street

Opened Oct. 16th, 1907, under the able management of David Belasco, with David Warfield in "The Grand Army Man." This was followed with Blanche Bates in "The Fighting Hope." "The Easiest Way," with Frances Starr in the leading role. The theatre is cozy and comfortable. A chime of bells, instead of an orchestra, is a striking feature of this theatre.

BETWEEN THE ACTS LITTLE CIGARS
ALL TOBACCO NO PAPER
NOT A CIGARETTE
Particularly satisfactory to smokers of High grade Cigars when time is limited.
THEATRES OLD AND NEW SERIES.

Cigarette packages offered pictures of actresses, sports heroes, and national parks to customers, but only miniature cigars featured New York theaters. [c.1910]

Cigar Cards Go Broadway

Until World War I, cigars were the primary form of tobacco use, and Between the Acts offered a way to blend two sociable experiences. [c.1910]

MAXINE ELLIOTT'S THEATRE,
39th St., Between Broadway and 6th Ave., New York

Is a fine example of Louis XVI style of architecture. It is consistent throughout and in keeping with the character of plays produced—refined modern comedy—and promises to be one of the favorite playhouses of New York. Was opened January, 1909, with "The Chaperon," under the management of George Appleton.

FACTORY NO 649 1ST DIST. N.Y.

BETWEEN THE ACTS LITTLE CIGARS
ALL TOBACCO NO PAPER
NOT A CIGARETTE
Particularly satisfactory to smokers of High grade Cigars when time is limited.
THEATRES OLD AND NEW SERIES.

MAXINE ELLIOTT'S THEATRE
NEW YORK
OPENED JANUARY 1909
MAXINE ELLIOTT'S THEATRE
MAXINE ELLIOTT'S THEATRE

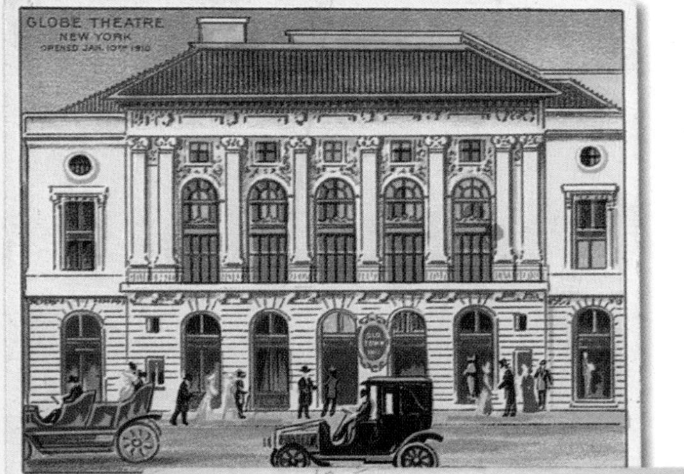

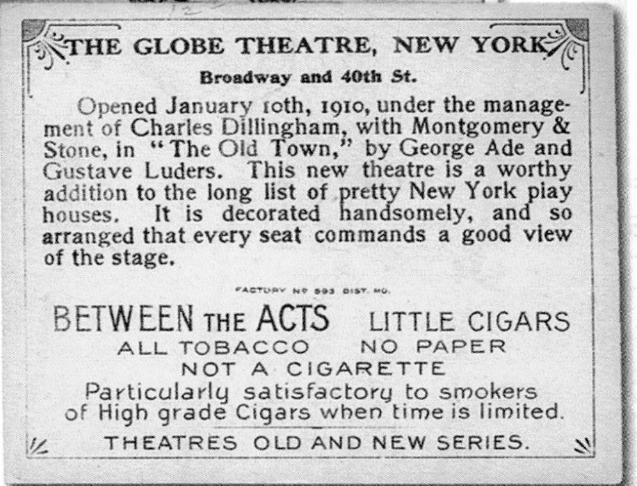

THE GLOBE THEATRE, NEW YORK

Broadway and 40th St.

Opened January 10th, 1910, under the management of Charles Dillingham, with Montgomery & Stone, in "The Old Town," by George Ade and Gustave Luders. This new theatre is a worthy addition to the long list of pretty New York play houses. It is decorated handsomely, and so arranged that every seat commands a good view of the stage.

FACTORY Nº 593 DIST. MO.

BETWEEN THE ACTS LITTLE CIGARS
ALL TOBACCO NO PAPER
NOT A CIGARETTE
Particularly satisfactory to smokers of High grade Cigars when time is limited.
THEATRES OLD AND NEW SERIES.

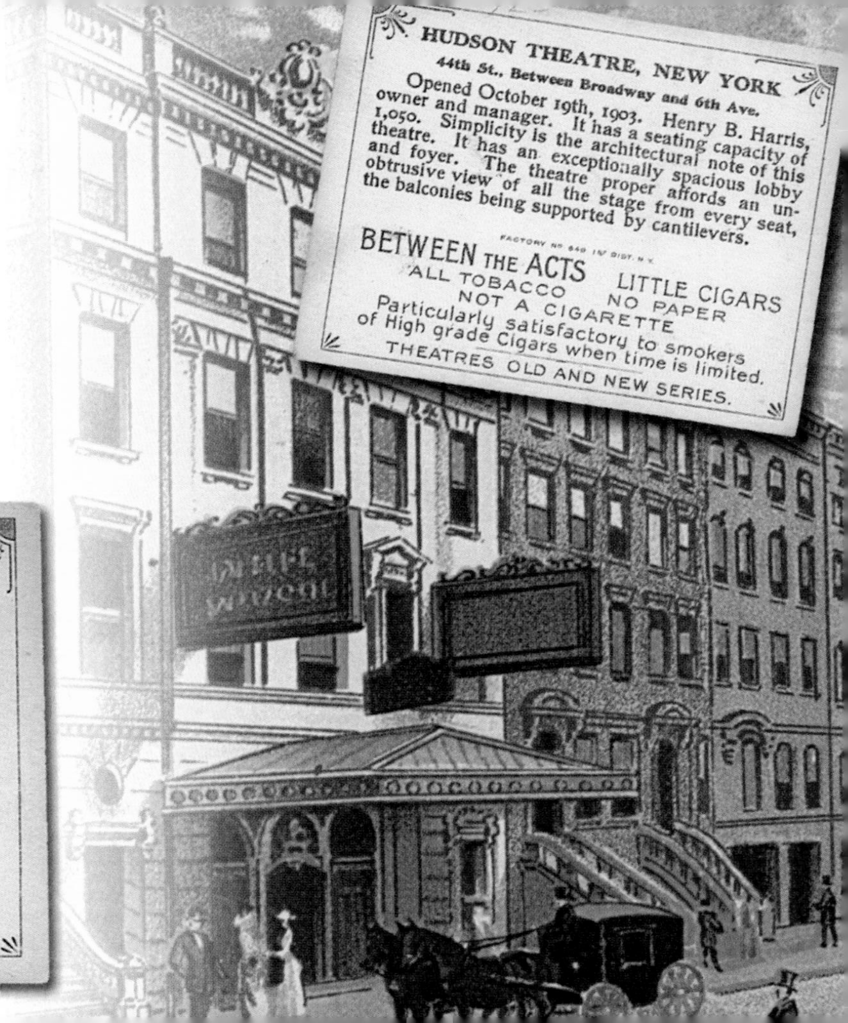

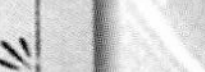

HUDSON THEATRE, NEW YORK

44th St., Between Broadway and 6th Ave.

Opened October 19th, 1903. Henry B. Harris, owner and manager. It has a seating capacity of 1,050. Simplicity is the architectural note of this theatre. It has an exceptionally spacious lobby and foyer. The theatre proper affords an unobtrusive view of all the stage from every seat, the balconies being supported by cantilevers.

FACTORY Nº 649 1ST DIST. N.Y.

BETWEEN THE ACTS LITTLE CIGARS
ALL TOBACCO NO PAPER
NOT A CIGARETTE
Particularly satisfactory to smokers of High grade Cigars when time is limited.
THEATRES OLD AND NEW SERIES.

The Winter Garden (1911) grew from the American Horse Exchange, and critics argued that bad shows rekindled the smell. The theater eventually hosted *Cats* for eighteen years and 7,485 performances. [c.1917]

The Hippodrome, the world's largest theater, opened in April 1905 to bring theater to "the masses." By 1906, its owners, the creators of Luna Park on Coney Island, had lost control of the theater. [c.1909]

The "department store of theatricals," the Hippodrome specialized in spectacles for a public that arrived by elevated train. It closed in 1939, a victim of the Depression. [c.1906]

Left: The Cort, although on the "wrong side" of Broadway, has been a lucky theater since Laurette Taylor opened there in 1912. [c.1912]

Right: The Lyceum is perhaps Times Square's most beautiful playhouse. [c.1903]

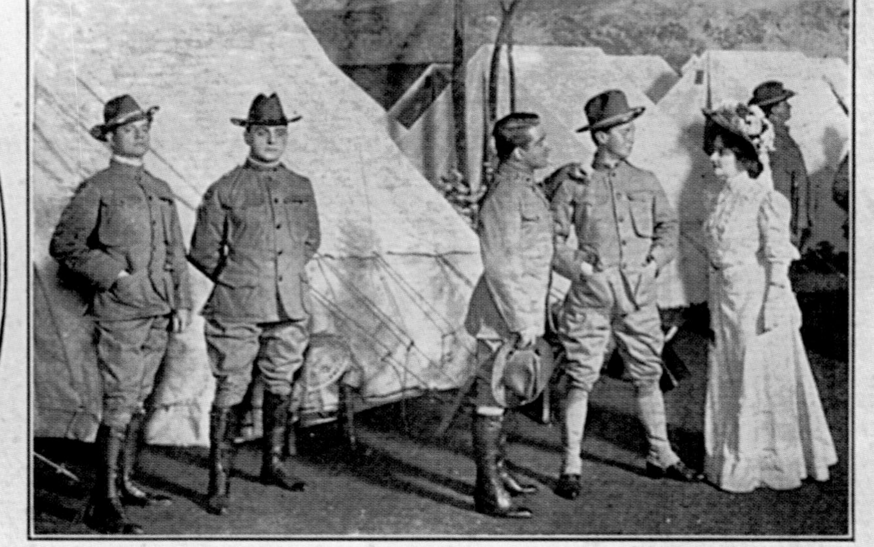

The Lyceum (1903) is Times Square's oldest active theater. Both its exterior and interior are landmarks. For forty years, impresario Daniel Frohman lived above the stage he managed. [c.1914]

Built in Italianate Florentine style and reminiscent of a bell tower, the *Times* Tower outshone the Venetian *Herald* building on 34th Street and dominated its surroundings. [c.1906]

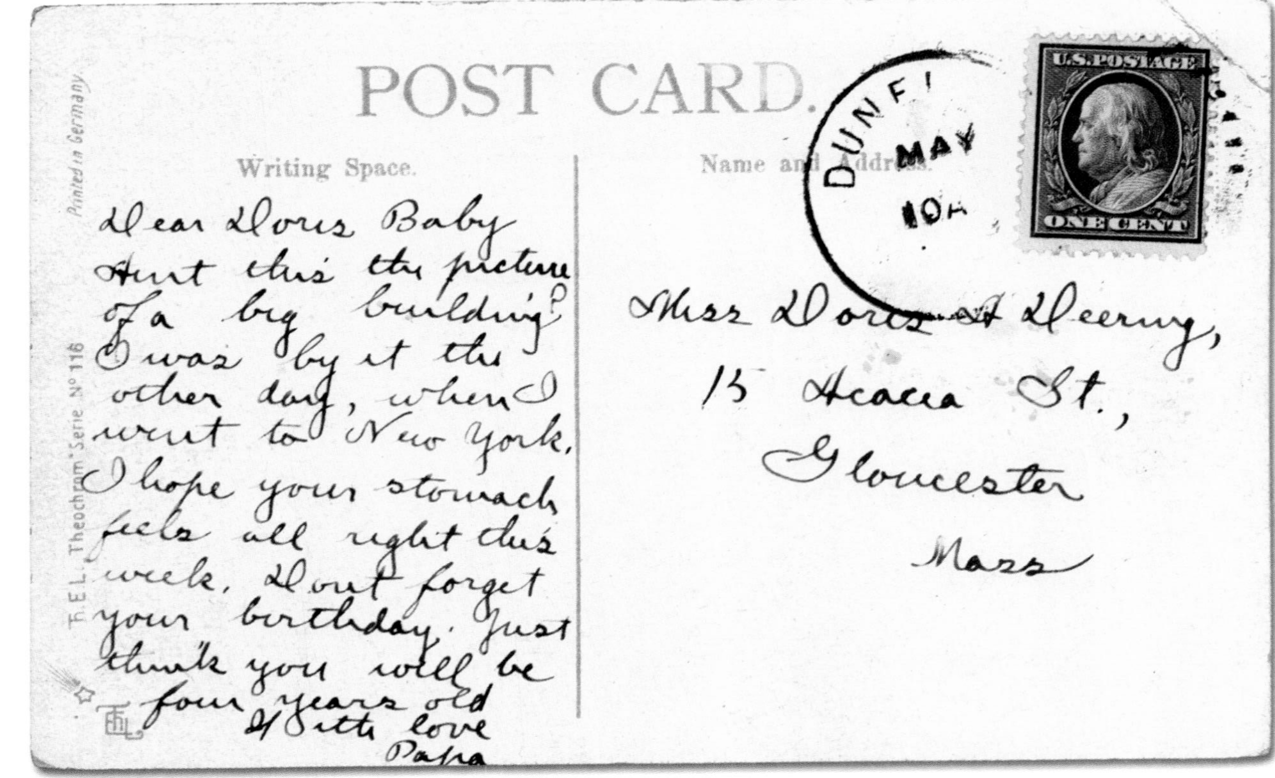

POST CARD.

Writing Space.

Dear Doris Baby
Aint this the picture
of a big building?
I was by it the
other day, when I
went to New York.
I hope your stomach
feels all right this
week. Don't forget
your birthday. Just
think you will be
four years old
With love
Papa

Name and Address.

Miss Doris A Deering,
15 Acacia St.,
Gloucester
Mass

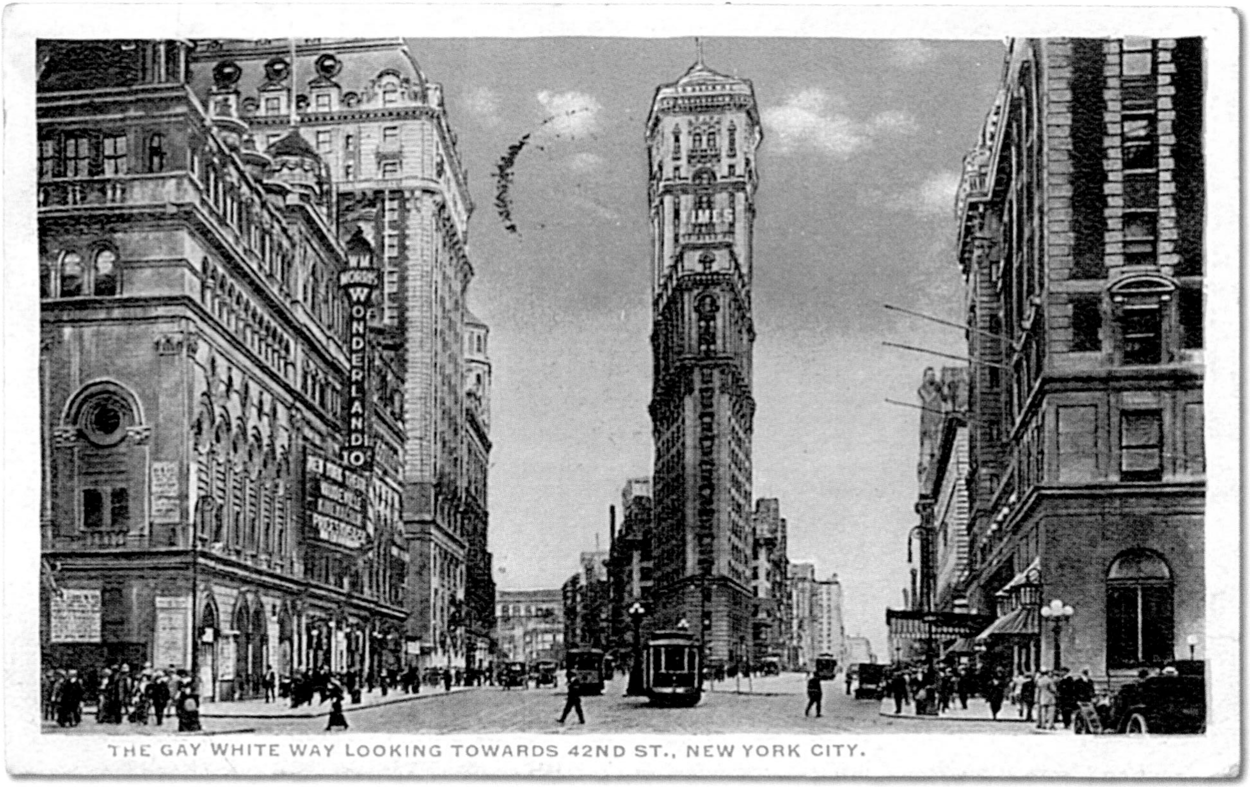
WM MORRIS
WONDERLAND
10
THE GAY WHITE WAY LOOKING TOWARDS 42ND ST., NEW YORK CITY.

Rooftop gardens, such as those atop Wonderland and the Astor Hotel, helped make Times Square "the Coney Island of America." [c.1915]

Times Square Bldg., New York.
TIMES BUILDING, situated at 42nd and Broadway, home of the New York Times, which was founded in 1851. New building erected in 1904-1905.

Post Card

NEW YORK
AUG 28
7 30 PM
1913

For Address only

Dear. Miss Ellis
You may be surprised to hear from me and hoping you may not think that we have lost our friendship I was not able to communicate with you till at the present time I was traveling all the time I told my room mate to write you that I could not come that sunday night of which I feel very sorry. Your Friend Y.M.C.A.
P. de Vries. 215 W 23rd St. New York City

Miss. Hazel Ellis
Ocean St.
Southington
Conn

The beaux-arts New York Public Library (1911) is one of the most beautiful buildings in America. Extensive renovations have modernized access to its immensely valuable research collections. [c.1915]

Dear Sara
Well here we are
in N.Y. Jane and I
and we are very busy
Jane has nearly
bought out Woolworths
Store buying things
for all these
Neices and Nephews
We have a very nice
room for 1.10 each a
day and running
hot Water and cold
and Ict Water in
the Hall

PLACE STAMP HERE

POSTCARD

THIS SPACE FOR ADDRESS ONLY

MANHATTAN CARD PUB. CO.

137

PUBLIC LIBRARY, New York. Public Library located on 5th Avenue and 42nd Street. Covers two entire city blocks, is built entirely of marble and cost nine million dollars. Opened for public use May 23, 1911, and contains over two million volumes and is said to be the most complete library in the country.

The perspective from the steps of the New York Public Library, looking north and west, shows the growing, fast-paced metropolis—as it does even today. [c.1915.]

The Eastern Edge

Fifth Avenue is the eastern border of the Times Square district, and its style is rather different from the glitter of the entertainment center. Its merchants are more expensive, its signs hug the fronts of buildings, and its restaurants are traditionally more sedate. Yet it was at Sherry's, on Fifth Avenue and 43rd Street, that Cornelius Kingsley Garrison Billings held a famed "Dinner on Horseback" in March 1903 to mark the completion of his racing stable. Despite such excess, in July 1907, elegant Fifth Avenue banned horse-drawn omnibuses from its precincts.

New York has always fought a losing battle with its traffic, and the gradual replacement of horse cars by automobiles, trolleys, and metered cabs (1907) greatly improved the odor of the entire district. In addition to banning horse-drawn vehicles, Fifth Avenue was first to install high traffic towers, which gave policemen a fighting chance to direct and survive the traffic; they soon obtained the ability to manually control the stop and go signals. But it was in Times Square that the first automated traffic signals in the United States went into operation in 1924. Traffic on Broadway, Seventh Avenue, and Fifth Avenue ran in two directions until well after mid-century, but today, the still horrible traffic runs only southward.

Two blocks east of the *Times* Tower, establishing a solid corner for the Times Square district, is perhaps the best-known landmark of Times Square's eastern edge—the huge mass of the New York Public Library. Created by the consolidation of three private collections in 1895, the library needed a permanent home for its multiple resources. To meet its demands, the antiquated Egyptian-style water reservoir that stood on 42nd Street was demolished between 1899 and 1902 to allow construction of the library. Designed by John Carrère and Thomas Hastings, the facility at Fifth Avenue and 42nd Street opened to the public on May 23, 1911, and is one of the five greatest research libraries in the world. All who visit the library must pass the two great lions who guard its entrance. To this day, native New Yorkers wait in eager expectation for Patience and Fortitude to roar—an occurrence that, according to legend, will take place only when a virgin passes.

Before traffic lights were installed in the 1920s, police directed traffic first by hand, and then by signs. Traffic towers helped them survive the vehicles they endeavored to control. [c.1915]

Managed by the Muschenheim brothers, the Astor was Times Square's favorite rendezvous spot for decades. Jimmy Durante occupied a fourth floor apartment for over twenty years. [c.1911]

POST CARD

U.S. POSTAGE ONE CENT

NEW YORK, N.Y. STA. N FEB 6 1 - PM 1911

THIS SPACE MAY BE USED FOR COMMUNICATION.

THE ADDRESS ONLY TO BE WRITTEN HERE.

Doesn't this make
you homesick? I
came on for one
week, nearly three
weeks ago - and
am still here!
Hate to leave -
Isabel Fay -

Mrs Frank S. Fay
3 Bellevue Street -
Worcester -
Mass.

50 S 30

HOTEL TIMES SQUARE, NEW YORK CITY
255 West 43rd Street, Just West of Broadway
1,000 Outside Rooms

Single with running water	$2.00	per day
Single with connecting bath	$2.25	" "
Single with private bath	$2.50–$3.00	" "
Double with running water (for two)	$3.00	" "
Double with private bath (for two)	$3.50–$4.00	" "
Combination of two rooms with bath between (for four)	$6.00–$7.00	" "

NO HIGHER RATES

Left: Postcard advertising documents Times Square's wide choice of hotels. The area is still the most "hoteled" part of New York, although rates have slightly increased over the years. [c.1909]

Right: The "Best People on Earth," members of the Benevolent and Protective Order of Elks, often stayed in the Times Square lodge. [c.1913]

The Grand Hotels of Times Square

As the Times Square area grew, the wealth of entertainment possibilities it offered demanded the construction of lodging facilities. This fact did not escape the notice of the Astor family, which, well versed in the possibilities of Manhattan development, seized the opportunity to open the two finest hotels in the district.

First, William Waldorf Astor decided that an elegant hostelry, modestly named for his family, would rise on the block between 44th and 45th Streets. Designed by Clinton and Russell in a French Renaissance style, the eleven-floor Astor Hotel opened to general acclaim on September 9, 1904. It featured a mansard roof, where a garden restaurant attracted elite diners; elegant drinking dens such as the Indian Hall Grill and the Hunt Room; and impeccable service provided by Ferdinand and William Muschenheim. The Astor hosted diplomatic missions and the Carnegie peace delegates, and was the starting point for the New York to Paris Auto Race of 1908. For decades, it was the site for both the Debutantes and the Beaux Arts Balls, held innumerable conventions, and entertained nine incumbent United States presidents. Demolished between 1967 and 1968, only the address—One Astor Plaza—remains of its glory.

But the second Astor project may still be glimpsed at the southeast corner of Broadway and 42nd Street. The French Renaissance exterior of the Knickerbocker Hotel was in fact completed before the Astor, but when its builders ran out of money, John Jacob Astor IV stepped in to complete the interior. When the Knickerbocker opened in October 1906, it had 556 rooms, restaurants capable of seating 2,000, and Maxwell Parrish's famous "Old King Cole" mural in its first floor bar. Very quickly, the Knickerbocker became "New York's country club." Both George M. Cohan and Enrico Caruso lived there, and the latter often entertained guests with an aria after returning from work at the Metropolitan Opera, two blocks away. The Knickerbocker was so successful that it purchased the adjacent hotel and incorporated its rooms in 1911. But Prohibition destroyed its prosperity, and in the 1920s, it was converted into offices; its King Cole mural was moved to the St. Regis Hotel in 1935.

Modern Times Square is the most "hoteled" district in the city, offering accommodations ranging from Holiday Inns to Hiltons, and from Victorian elegance to post-modern glitz. But if visitors wish to recapture a bit of early Times Square, they may do so by gazing at the still lovely Renaissance façade of the old Knickerbocker Hotel.

Hotels competed fiercely for clientele. The Bristol identified East Side hotels and Madison Square landmarks, but ignored the presence of the Astor on Broadway. [c.1916] ▶

HOTEL BRISTOL

122-124 WEST 49TH STREET
NEW YORK

ONE BLOCK EAST OF BROADWAY, IN THE VERY CENTRE OF THE THEATRES, WITHIN EASY WALKING DISTANCE OF ALL SHOPS, AND CONVENIENT TO ALL LINES OF TRANSPORTATION.

ROOMS WITH RUNNING WATER, $1.50 PER DAY
ROOMS WITH PRIVATE BATH, $2.00 PER DAY
SUITES, $8.00 PER DAY

T. E. TOLSON
PRES. & MGR.

HOTEL BRISTOL

PENN. R.R. STATION

ASTOR THEATRE

BROADWAY

SEVENTH AVE

AVE

49TH STREET

30116

VALENTINE-SOUVENIR CO. N.Y.

MANHATTAN HOTEL — BELMONT HOTEL — MADISON SQUARE GARDEN — METROPOLITAN LIFE TOWER — TIMES BUILDING — HAMMERSTEIN'S THEA

The dominance of the *Times* Tower over its surroundings is apparent in this advertising postcard issued by the Woodstock Hotel. [c.1916]

Restaurants of Times Square

New York has always been a city that loves to eat well. Since each previous entertainment center had featured exceptional dining, it was certain that Times Square would draw entrepreneurs eager to satisfy the appetites of the theater crowd. It was not that food was unattainable in Longacre Square; fresh lobster, oyster bars flaunting red and white balloon signs, and drinking spots offering free Hudson River caviar already dotted the area. But theatergoers demanded a finer dining experience—one that might include the thrill of rubbing shoulders with the "swells," gamblers, and performers found in the "Rialto." Theater habitués known as Champagne Charlie's and Stagedoor Johnny's were always common along the Great White Way of theaters, and New Yorkers were thrilled at the news that every original Florodora girl married a millionaire. The middle class audience targeted by restaurateurs wanted dinner to be more than food; it also wanted a show.

The first salvos of the dining battle were fired during the 1890s on Fifth Avenue and 44th Street, where Richard Canfield had opened a casino. Canfield's patrons demanded the best food in town, and two heavyweight restaurants fought to provide it. Delmonico's opened right next door, boasting that it had invented fine dining in the metropolis, and creating dishes such as Lobster Newburg and Baked Alaska for its guests. "Diamond Jim" Brady admitted that he stationed himself five inches from a Delmonico's table, and stopped eating only when his stomach touched wood. But Louis Sherry rose to the challenge, hiring Stanford White to build an elegant restaurant/hotel diagonally across from Delmonico's. Sherry's catered the famous "Dinner on Horseback" for the New York Riding Club in 1903. The two giants battled for supremacy on Fifth Avenue until Prohibition.

In Longacre Square, opulent dining began when Rector's opened for business next to the Olympia complex on September 23, 1899. After spending half a million dollars and installing the first revolving door in Manhattan, the "Sign of the Green Dolphin" brought French cuisine to Manhattan's new entertainment center. Rector's private rooms and more discreet gambling facilities soon drew "Diamond Jim" and his crowd, even as management

Restaurants of Times Square

struggled to keep out chorus girls searching for a nightly "sugar daddy." George Rector's competition first came from Thomas Shanley, who moved his Empire Room north from 23rd Street and opened a "lobster palace" on the west side of Seventh Avenue. The two competed for customers on opposite sides of the rising *Times* Tower. In short order, the roster of competitors included Churchill's, Maxim's, the Metropole Café, and the Café d'Opera, as well as Barbetta's, the first Italian restaurant in the area. When the roof gardens on the Olympia, the Casino, and Hammerstein's Victoria were added to the mix, a wondrous variety of options became available for pre- or post-theater dining.

Fine dining was also pledged by Times Square hotels. The Astor offered the Hunt Room, and the Knickerbocker touted its Grill as part of a total Times Square experience. Some area hotels were little more than brothels, but these establishments promised luxury accommodations and unparalleled service in quiet surroundings. Serenity was important, since the subway deposited 5 million people annually into the area after 1905, and a quarter million passed through it on a daily basis. The opening of Pennsylvania Station (1911) and Grand Central Terminal (1913) only increased congestion, making a quiet dining experience all the more desirable.

From 1899 to 1919, Rector's set the standard for fine dining in Times Square. George M. Cohan's work studio was above the restaurant's 43rd Street location. [c.1909]

On 42nd Street itself, the opening of a succession of new theaters created the opportunity for yet another gustatory adventure. In 1908, Murray's Roman Gardens opened for business, perhaps the most sumptuous of all Times Square eateries. Designer Henri Erkins created a wonderland of statues and fountains, and even a revolving floor. Reviewers praised service and cuisine that was "almost perfect," and style that befitted a "cabaret for the people." Murray's was a fixture on 42nd Street until 1925, when it was replaced by Hubert's Flea Circus; the space is now filled by Madame Tussaud's Wax Museum.

In retrospect, the great age of Times Square restaurants was ended by the great Prohibition experiment. Only one institution of that age endured far beyond the 1920s. The Horn & Hardart Automat opened on Broadway and 46th Street on July 12, 1912, with catering by Sherry's. A self-service emporium created by two Philadelphia merchants, the Automat provided generations of diners with the best baked beans, fish cakes, and buns in the city; its 5-cent cup of coffee lasted until 1952. In Times Square, the fast food pioneer collected 8,693 nickels on its first day of operation, and was the prototype for fifty other Automats that followed. The last Automat closed in 1991, and a part of New York's history vanished forever. Hundreds of restaurants would open and close in the theater district over the years, but dining, both ordinary and extraordinary, was never as adventurous as when Times Square was being born.

The Allied Chemical Tower

After 1913, most operations of "The New York Times" were centered in West 43rd Street, but the newspaper's distinctive tower remained the focal point of Times Square. Not until 1961 did the Times sell the building, most fittingly to Douglas Leigh, whose signs of perfect smoke rings and waterfalls had enlivened the area for a quarter century. Leigh saw the tower as a prime advertising site, and sold it five years later to Allied Chemical, which installed a distinctive marble skin. But Allied found the location cramped, and sold it to Alexander Parker, who called his property One Times Square (1975). The tower has since changed hands several times, always at a profit. Its present value is determined by the signs it holds, rather than the memories it evokes.

In the 1960s, the new Allied Chemical Tower failed to revive a district tumbling into disorder. [c.1967]

Even in 2000, signs on the tower (left) and the Knickerbocker Hotel (right) played an important role in Times Square.

CHAPTER FOUR

Resurrection, 1975–2000

By the mid-1970s, New York was a city in turmoil. For 150 years, it had been the financial and industrial center of the nation, the most wealthy urban center in the United States. But in a single decade, the metropolis lost over 600,000 manufacturing jobs and its finances were shattered by a mountain of debt. When it reluctantly sought federal aid, its pleas were met with only disdain. The famous *Daily News* headline of 1975—"Ford to City, Drop Dead"—summarized the situation in a nutshell.

Even at its lowest point, Times Square never lacked advocates who believed it could recapture its lost prominence. In 1978, the 42nd Street Redevelopment Corporation made a modest start on the road back with a plan to upgrade several off-Broadway theaters located west of Eighth Avenue. Created with the backing of New York State, the corporation argued that conditions had actually improved since the mid-1960s, and that the swing of the historical pendulum was already apparent. Edward Koch took office as mayor that January, and his faith in the city provided additional momentum through the Office of Midtown Planning and the City Planning Department. Many ideas were presented for the upgrading of the area—raising a domed pedestrian shopping center and creating a "Combat Zone" where bawdiness could be contained—but the first priority was leadership. Fortunately, Broadway theaters were in the midst of three successive good years in receipts—1976 to 1978—and the housing complex called Manhattan Plaza opened with such a long waiting list of applications that it assured population stability. Among many reports was a university study which demonstrated that 42nd Street was not a "ghetto street." Supporters seemed to agree that "the Bright Light District is a permanent world's fair which only awaits its main attractions to be successful."

None of the surveys implied that the task of reconstruction would be easy. The reality was that much of Times Square's vigor, and even the quality of its lights, had been drained away by years of neglect. Electricity and neon had long characterized the area, but the energy crisis of the 1970s and the subsequent economic turndown forced advertisers to create signs using computer-generated reflective vinyl rather than more expensive systems. It was symbolic of commercial failure that the most attractive and innovative animated sign of the decade advertised the Pussy Cat Lounge. American advertisers seemed to shun the area, and in the 1980s, Times Square succumbed to what was termed the "Japanese invasion." As American manufacturers lost their drive, signs for SONY, Canon, Seiko, Fuji, Casio, Minolta, Ricoh, Sanyo, Aiwa, and Konica dominated. Even Douglas Leigh, the sign maker most identified with neon's glory age in the 1950s, left Times Square to concentrate on other facets of his business. In 1979, Leigh disposed of his valued billboard space in a deal with the Van Wagner Company. Thus as Midtown South reported the largest number of felonies in New York in 1978, and feminists marched through the streets in a War Against Pornography in 1979, one of the area's heroic figures appeared to be jumping ship. The need to reclaim Times Square before it sank forever was increasingly clear.

Like many conflicts, the crusade began with a defeat. The venerable Astor Hotel had been levelled in 1969, and replaced by an uninviting office building. Times Square, once the hotel center of the city, had not added new hotel space in seven decades—another reason for its decline. Responding to the opportunity, the Marriott Corporation acquired the block between 45th and 46th Streets, and hired John Portman to design a major new hostel. The new structure—the Marriott Marquis, completed in 1985—would demolish the Astor and Victoria Theaters, as well as the world's largest sign, which stretched over the two movie palaces. Moreover, despite long courtroom proceedings, the Helen Hayes Theater on the side street also would fall before the wreckers. These losses inspired a strong city preservationist movement, already in full cry because of the destruction of Penn Station. In subsequent years, the interiors and exteriors of forty-five theaters would become designated landmarks, guaranteeing that valued Times Square institutions would no longer be at risk.

One key to the renewal was the creation of a Special Midtown Zoning District. Times Square had grown haphazardly over the years, but if the seediness of sex shops was to be eliminated, direction from the city was needed. Hearings on the new district began in 1982, and immediately generated at least fifty-nine lawsuits against all proposed changes. None of these suits would be successful. As hearings proceeded, zoning amendments were finalized. Times Square, the heart of the Theater Sub-District Core Area, was recognized as a unique "advertising park" demanding lights and color. The 1987 code mandated that the first 120 feet of building façade *must* be designed to accommodate illuminated signs, and that new construction must house lively ground floor operations. Under the spur of the new regulations, spectacular signs, reduced to only fourteen in 1984, reappeared, eventually to number beyond fifty.

The obvious commitment of the city and developers to Times Square encouraged the business community to reevaluate the potential of the area. Another hotel, the Crown Plaza, began to rise in 1986, and during the 1990s, Times Square again became the most heavily roomed area of Manhattan. Embassy Suites, Hilton, Millennium, Macklowe, Renaissance, and Sofitel opened new facilities, and many more were planned for future construction. Major corporations—Virgin, Disney, and Warner Brothers—opened in the area as well, once more making it family-friendly. The decade of the 1990s proved to be one of the most profitable in theater history, if not the most innovative, as long-running shows dominated the marquees of Times Square. In 2000, 38.5 million tourists visited New York, and once again, Times Square was an essential stop on their travels. Magic had been restored to the "Crossroads of the World."

During the 1980s, signs announcing the "Japanese invasion" filled Times Square, providing the advertising revenue needed to spur development. [c.1985]

Gaudy signs, sex shows, and fast food restaurants marked the transition stage in the recovery of Times Square. [c.1985]

By the mid-1980s, Times Square was surrounded by high buildings, creating a canyon-like effect. [c.1985]

Though only metal piping, canvas, and a box, the TKTS booth tremendously stimulated the revival of Times Square. [c.1994]

Rebuilding Times Square

In 1984, with typical New York modesty, Mayor Ed Koch announced that New York City would begin the "greatest building project since the pyramids"—the redevelopment of Times Square. The scenario called for the construction of four new office towers at the south end of the square, a merchandising center, one new hotel, subway improvements, and the restoration of nine theaters on 42nd Street. Koch claimed that the Prudential-led consortium would have full cooperation from both city and state, but many observers, mistrustful of his administration's long association with developers, condemned the grandiosity of the proposal. Needless to say, like so many New York plans, this one was never carried out as proposed. However, it did become the starting point for the last transformation that Times Square would undergo in the twentieth century.

As Prudential Insurance and developer George Klein soon discovered, critics believed that the scale of their proposals threatened the historic "style" of the Times Square area. The initial design that emerged, created by Philip Johnson and John Burgee, placed four massive granite towers at the south end of the square. Not even mansard roofs with glass elements could lessen their bulk, and it was believed that they would cast long shadows over the activity below. Critical and public outrage forced a return to the drawing board, and when the redesign appeared in 1992, the buildings' relationship to the center of the square had been reassessed. Their bulk, however, remained unchanged. Moreover, Prudential officials were having second thoughts because of a perceived surplus of New York office space. As controversy over the southern blueprint continued, less ambitious redevelopment began by fits and starts at the northern end of the disputed territory.

Perhaps the only constant in two decades of planning a new Times Square was a desire to maintain the aura and ambience of the district. The entertainment Rialto had always been identified with bright lights, frenzied activity, and commercial advertising, and the zoning amendments passed in the 1980s were aimed in that historical direction. If Venice would never cover its canals, Times Square would not dim its lights. But new construction like the Marriott and the Crown Plaza hotels failed to add much to the gaiety. The rising new building at 1585 Broadway and 47th Street thus became a test of the new requirements. A forty-two-story office tower on the site of the Strand Theater, the building did have electric signs on its frontage, but when it opened in 1989, it became a real estate white elephant. From 1990 to 1995, it held but a single tenant, the prominent law firm of Proskauer Rose, and lost almost $2 million monthly. Purchased by Morgan Stanley in the summer of 1993, it was transformed into an object of constant motion when the world's largest LED display was placed on its façade. Three tickers with ten-foot-high letters moved continually across its front, offering the latest market news. Within a year, the disaster was transformed into a bulwark of the emerging new Times Square. Soon joined by the Renaissance Hotel, 750 Seventh Avenue, and a new hotel designed by Fox and Fowle placed above the Palace Theater, the north end of Times Square suddenly had a very new appearance. Moreover, the German media conglomerate Bertelsmann located itself in the center of action by occupying the vital block from 45th to 46th Streets. When commercial risk takers like the Gap and Virgin Atlantic took advantage of temporarily declining rental rates to open new outlets in Times Square itself, it became apparent that the tide was changing.

And then came Disney. Everyone concerned with the redevelopment process understood that so long as 42nd Street remained "Sin Street," new construction would have little effect. But constant governmental pressure, driven by the ever-growing number of visitors to New York, had finally succeeded in reducing the prominence of sex shops along "the Deuce." Placing faith in a continuation of that effort, on the last day of Mayor David Dinkins' term—December 31, 1993—the Disney Corporation signed an agreement to refurbish the venerable but long-abandoned New Amsterdam Theater as its New York showplace. Moreover, it would open a retail outlet on the corner of Seventh Avenue and Broadway to draw family shoppers into the area. Additional negotiations with the administration of Rudolph Giuliani were necessary before the final contracts were signed, but the commitment of Disney seemed to promise a new 42nd Street. The Livant Corporation and MTV announced that they, too, would enter formerly forbidding sidewalks. Soon Forest City Ratner joined in to redevelop the southwestern part of the street. Most sex stores were eliminated by 1998, new theaters and movies were opened, Madame Tussaud's brought in wax dummies to replace prostitutes, and by the end of the millennium, "the Deuce" had regained its original prominence as a showplace.

In 1996, developer Douglas Durst purchased from Prudential the right to develop the "Corner" at the northeastern intersection of 42nd Street and Broadway. Durst's faith in the economic future fostered construction of 4 Times Square, the Condé Nast tower designed by Fox and Fowle. Its façade advertises NASDAQ with the world's largest and most complex digital sign, a creation that by itself returns $2 million annually to the Durst coffers. In 1997, the Rudin Group acquired development rights for a second Prudential site; the Reuters Building at 3 Times Square is the fourth Fox and Fowle building on the new square. In 1998, the Pru sold off its last two development sites, recapturing its original investment—and probably happy to leave the real estate market it had never mastered. So rapid was the pace of development that the Disney Store, which contributed so much to the revival of 42nd Street, was later sacrificed to the wrecking ball. Perhaps most important, as new towers rise within the Times Square area, they will continue to add light to the scene.

These few paragraphs can hardly convey the extraordinary changes that Times Square experienced in the last decade of the twentieth century. In a way, the saga is one that justifies America's faith in an undirected marketplace. Entrepreneurial decisions drove the revival, and by 2000, there were over a quarter of a million workers who came to the area daily. These were joined by hordes of visitors, both domestic and foreign, for most of the anticipated dangers of Times Square had been eliminated. Moreover, the fear that huge office towers would darken the entertainment center proved foolish, for the lights of the Great White Way have never been brighter. There are now manmade "canyons" that surround Times Square, but they cast no shadows over its activity. Even at high noon, a vast array of colors dominates the eye in a way technically impossible even twenty years ago. Times Square has not only become a commercial success, but has also become the center of America's media life. Although much changed, it remains the heart of New York.

A vast food court leads to multiplex entertainment on the north side of the new 42nd Street.

TKTS is one of the most popular structures on Times Square, for it offers half-price tickets to theatergoers.

The Saga of the Empire Theater

On September 11, 1912, the Eltinge Theater, designed by the great Thomas Lamb and named in honor of Broadway's leading female impersonator, opened for business at 236 West 42nd Street. Constructed by Albert Woods in partnership with Julian Eltinge (1883–1944), the new playhouse featured beaux-arts decor. Eltinge garnered a nice income from the theater's operations and used it to finance some of his colorful escapades. His reported quip, "My life is one close shave after another," neatly summarized his bizarre lifestyle.

Small and intimate in size, with 759 seats, the Eltinge was one of the more successful theaters on "The Deuce"—until the Depression. A famous mural depicting its namesake as three Muses was added shortly before the theater was converted into a burlesque house. The ensuing mayoral campaign against burlesque forced it to become a "grinder" showing B-movies, and it staggered on into the 1950s as the Laff Movie Theater. Changing its name to the Empire in 1954 hardly altered its dismal prospects.

Because of its small size and years of neglect, the Empire was not considered a primary candidate for restoration when the 42nd Street Redevelopment Corporation was formed. But the power of its still elegant façade and the rediscovery of the painted-over Eltinge mural changed its fate. In 1998, the Eltinge-Empire—all 7.4 million pounds of it—was placed on jacks and moved 169 feet to the west. Totally renovated by Forest City Ratner Companies, it reopened in April 2000 as the entry to the twenty-five-screen AMC Empire multiplex, offering first-run, independent, and even "adrenaline" movies of the kung fu and chase genres. The theater boasts four roof decks, where visitors can sun, smoke, view some of the city, and perhaps dream of Ziegfeld's roof garden. Like so many of the area's landmarks, it seems to prove that if you wait, Times Square will make use of you.

After traveling 169 feet west, the Empire Theater reopened as a multiplex.

Since 1996, a half-size Concorde SST has soared in place over the world's most famous intersection.

CONCLUSION

An American Experience

The United States is a vast and complex nation, its 285 million people a mosaic of cultures and languages stretching over five time zones and proudly boasting a host of alternate lifestyles. States avidly compete with one another; regional differences are enthusiastically trumpeted; and urban, rural, and suburban tensions churn its politics. Yet all Americans know that their nation works, and that the entire world marvels at the power, strength, and unity of a country that should have self-destructed long ago. The genius of America is its ability to create unity out of its diversity, so the citizens of this hard-to-define nation justly celebrate the occasions when we act as one. We vote together on Election Day, celebrate our heritage of freedom on the Fourth of July, and mourn together when confronting tragedy. And it is not unlikely that on every New Year's Eve, we count down together as a nation, watching a mutltifaceted crystal ball drop down from the old *Times* Tower. More powerfully than Adolph Ochs could ever have imagined, the public meeting place he envisioned when he maneuvered to create Times Square in 1904 came into existence over the course of the twentieth century.

Modern Street Sign

For almost a hundred years, Times Square has been a place where things happen. Despite its identification with the theater and dining, movies and the news, it was never "just" an entertainment center. It was always a destination, a setting in which the face of America could be seen and studied. It belonged first of all to New Yorkers, then to Americans, and finally to the entire world. Its spectacular signs demonstrate the ingenuity of the advertiser, the range of American wealth, the intense need to market a product that can easily be displaced tomorrow. The range of its entertainments—from legitimate stage to peepshow, from epic film to bawdy burlesque, from arcade to architecture—is unrivaled anywhere. It remains today as it was in the heyday of Hammerstein and Ochs, the place to go in Manhattan. The Times Square subway station is still first in usage among the 468 stations in New York City, and the crowds that fill the world's crossroads are still overwhelming. Most of

Broadway will continue to put its best foot forward into the new millennium [c.1990]

the 39 million tourists who visit the Big Apple each year find their way into Times Square, and the congestion has become so great that the Giuliani Administration made plans to widen the sidewalks at the crossroads, reconfigure the traffic flow, and install more public toilets. Only the latter are truly important because Times Square will continue to impose itself on any small attempts to alter its reality.

Every generation of the century has used, abused, and changed Times Square. The contributions of each are still apparent if you look carefully, for wandering through its confines is a walk through history. The wonderful images and messages from the postcards in this volume enable us to recapture moments of Times Square's illustrious past, but they are only stills from a panorama that continues. New hotels, new corporations, and new stage productions may be the current reality of the area, but its attraction is deeper than the present moment. *The New York Times* is now printed in Queens and New Jersey, but it continues to maintain its presence in Times Square. For a century, the beating heart of the metropolis has been located there, drawing millions of tourists and native New Yorkers into its vital rhythm. Every visitor takes away something from simply passing through Times Square, but our own brief word and picture tour of America's playground is finished. Enjoy!

Index

All numbers that appear in blue type *indicate pages that include postcard images.*

A

A & P coffee cup sign, 72
Abe Lincoln in Illinois, 84
Academy of Music, 27
Adonis, 64
Advertising. *See* Commercialism.
Aiwa sign, 156
Allen, Woody, 76
Allied Chemical, 153
Allied Chemical Tower, 20, 151, 153
AMC Empire multiplex, 165
American Expeditionary Forces parade, 57
American Horse Exchange, 2, 28
American Souvenir Card Company, 6
American Theater, 28
"America's Acropolis." *See* Rockefeller Center.
America's Worst Act, 87
Ankles Aweigh, 144
Apollo Theater, 28
"Aquarium" sign, 70
Armed Forces Recruiting Station, 106
Artkraft Corporation, 20
Associated Press, 75
Astaires, the, 80
Astor, John Jacob, 2
Astor, John Jacob IV, 48
Astor, William Backhouse, 2
Astor, William Waldorf, 48
Astor Hotel, 9, 15, 16, 24, 39, 45, 48, 52, 118, 147, 150, 156

Astor Theater, 118, 156
Automat, Horn & Hardart, 52, 62, 96
Automobile Row, 99

Balboa, the, 106
Ball, the New Year's Eve, 19–20
Barbetta's restaurant, 52
Beatles, the, 69
Beaux Arts Ball, 48
Beck, Martin, 123
Belafonte, Harry, 123
Belmont, August, 19
Ben Hur, 71
Benevolent and Protective Order of Elks, 47
Bennet, Arnold, 71
Benny, Jack, 105
Benny Goodman Band, 105
Berle, Milton, 105
Berlin, Irving, 67, 87, 98
Bernays, Edward, 72
Bernhardt, Sarah, 87
Bertelsmann, 161
Between the Acts cigar advertisement, 30, 31
Billings, Cornelius Kingsley Garrison, 44
Birth of a Nation, 117
Bogart, Humphrey, 105
Bolger, Ray, 76, 80
Bond waterfall sign, 99, 131, 137
Boys of Company "B," The, 36
Brady, "Diamond Jim," 8, 51, 54
Brando, Marlon, 98
Brass Rail restaurant, 126
Brecker, Louis and Dorothy, 80
Brice, Fannie, 64, 87, 88
Bristol Hotel, 49
British Building, 75
Broadway, 7, 11. *See also* Theater; Theater District.
"Broadway Battleships," 28
Broadway Mob, 64
Bubbling Bromo sign, 72
Buick automobiles, 16
Buitoni Spaghetti Bar, 128
Burgee, John, 161
Burke, Billie, 67
Burlesque, 87–88

C

C & G Corsets sign, 71
Café d'Opera, 52
Camel sign, 72, 147
Can-Can, **143**
Canfield, Richard, 51
Canon sign, 156
Cantor, Eddie, 67, 88

Capitol Theater, 105, 118
Carousel, 98
Carrère, John, 44
Carroll, Earl, 85
Caruso, Enrico, 12, 48
Casa Manana, 64
Casablanca, 105
Casino de Paree, 64
Casino Theater, 1, 3, 27, 52
Casio sign, 156
"Cathedral of the Motion Picture," 118, 121
Cats, 32
CC Gingerale sign, 71
Central Park, 2
Central Powers, the, 6
Channel Island, 75
Cherry Sisters, 87
Chesterton, Lord, 71
Chevrolet sign, 72
Children's Hour, The, 83
Child's Restaurant, 69, 125
China, 105
Christmas tree at Rockefeller Center, 75, 141
Churchill's restaurant, 8, 52, 59, 130
Cigar cards, 30
Civil War, 2
Claridge Hotel, 72
Claude, Georges, 72
Clinton and Russell, 48
Cohan, George M., 48, 52, 149
Colombian Exposition (1893), 5
Colucci's Restaurant and Bar, 102
Columbus Day bobby-soxer riot, 105
Come Blow Your Horn, 98
Commercialism, 71–72
Concorde SST replica, 166
Condé Nast tower, 162
"Conrad and Graham," 87
Corps de Ballet, 76, 77
Cort Theatre, 35, 144
Corticelli Spool Silk sign, 17, 71
Costello, 64
Cowcatcher Building, 71
Crash of 1929, 64, 72, 75
Crater, Judge, 64
Criterion Theater, 26, 27, 117, 118
Crown Plaza hotel, 156, 161

Daily News, 155
Daly, Arnold, 36
Darrow, Clarence, 63
Davies, Marion, 67
Davis, Stuart, 76
Death of a Salesman, 98
Debutantes Ball, 48
Delmonico's restaurant, 8, 61, 63

Depression, effects of the, 16, 34, 63, 64, 72, 75, 76, 80, 83, 88, 97, 118, 165
Deskey, Donald, 76
"Deuce, the," 162, 165
Diamond Horseshoe, 64, 98
Dinkins, David, 162
"Dinner on Horseback," 44, 51
Disney Company, 28, 156, 162
Disney Store, 162
Dodge Brothers sign, 72
Doubletree Suites, 123
Dove, Billie, 67
Duffy, Francis X., 109
Duffy Square, 88, 149
Dunne, Irene, 67
Durant, William, 16
Durante, Jimmy, 45
Durst, Douglas, 162

E

Earl Carroll Theater, 64
Edward Rice Company, 71
Eidlitz, Cyrus, 19
Eighteenth Amendment, 63
Einstein, Izzy, 63
Eisenstaedt, Alfred, 106
Elevated railway lines, 4
Elks lodge, 47
Ellis Island, 97
Eltinge, Julian, 165
Eltinge Theater, 165
Eltinge-Empire Theater, 165
Embassy Suites, 123, 156
Empire Room, 52
Empire Theater (Charles Frohman's), 27
Empire Theater (formerly Eltinge Theater), 165
Erkins, Henri, 52
Erlanger, Abraham, 67, 87

F

"Famous Hollywood Cabaret" Restaurant, 81
Faust, 4
Fay, Larry, 64
Fifth Avenue Theater, 3
Fifth Season, The, 144
Flea Hop, 106
Florodora girls, 4, 51, 144
Follies. *See Ziegfeld Follies.*
Follies of 1907, 67
Ford, Henry, 16
Forest City Ratner, 162, 165
42nd Street (c. 1967), 151. *See also* "Sin Street."
42nd Street Redevelopment Corporation, 155, 165

43rd Street Merchant Seaman's Club, 111
"Fountain of Youth" mural, 76
Four Roses sign, 98
Fox and Fowle, 161, 162
Fox Corporation, 118
Franklin, Benjamin, 5
French, T. Henry, 28
French Building, 75
Friml, Rudolf, 67
Frohman, Charles, 27
Frohman, Daniel, 36
Fuji sign, 156

G

Gaity Theater, 4
Garland, Judy, 98, 123
Garrick Theater, 3
Gay White Way, 39, 68. *See also* Great White Way.
General Electric Building, 75
General Motors, 16
Gershwin, George, 67
Girl in the Red Velvet Swing, The, 87
Giuliani, Rudolph, 162
Globe Theatre, 31
Goddard, Paulette, 67
Goldsmith, Charles, 5
Goldwyn, Sam, 67
Gordon, "Waxy," 64
Gordon, Witold, 76
Grand Central Terminal, 4, 52
Granlund, Nils, 64
Great Depression. *See* Depression, effects of the.
Great Kill stream, 2
Great White Way, 17, 21, 28, 51, 71, 105, 148, 162. *See also* Times Square.
Greater New York, 4, 7
Gude, O. J., 8, 21, 71, 72
Guys and Dolls, 98, 146

H

Hammerstein I, Oscar, 7, 26, 27, 28, 87
Hammerstein II, Oscar, 98, 117
Hammerstein, Willie, 28, 87
Hammerstein's Roof Garden, 29
Harper's Weekly, 1
Hastings, Thomas, 44
Heatherbloom Petticoats sign, Miss, 21
Hector's restaurant, 146
Heinz pickle sign, 71
Held, Anna, 67
Helen Hayes Theater, 156
Hellman, Lillian, 83
Herald building, 37
Herald Square, 19, 27

Herts and Tallent, 28
Hilton, 48, 156
Hippodrome, 28, 33, 34
Hiroshima, 106
"History of Cosmetics" (Gordon), 76
"Hole, the," 147
Holiday Inn, 48
Hollywood Restaurant, 64
Holy Cross Church, 109
Hoover Typewriters sign, 72
Hope, Bob, 105
Horn & Hardart Automat, 52, 62, 96
Horse-drawn vehicles, banning of, 44
Hotel Bristol, 49
Hotel Dixie, 126
Hotel Edison, 92
Hotel President, 93
Hotel Taft, 118, 126
Hotel Victoria, 126
Hotelings kiosk, 20, 135
Hotsy Totsy Club, 64
Hubert's Flea Circus, 52, 147
Hudson Theatre, 31
Hudson-Fulton Celebration, 6
Hunt, Richard Morris, 3
Hunt Room drinking den, 48, 52
Hutton, Betty, 98

Iceman Cometh, The, 98
Indian Hall Grill, 48
Into the Woods, 168
IRT system, 20

Jack Dempsey's Restaurant
  first, 129
  second, 130
James, Harry, 69, 105
Japanese advertising, growth of, 156, 157
Jardin de Danse roof complex, 27
Jardin de Paris, 67
Jersey Bounce, 106
Jig Walk, 106
Jitterbug, 106
Joe Moss's International Casino, 64
Johnny Walker sign, 98
Johnson, Philip, 161
Jolson, Al, 80

Kaye, Danny, 98, 105, 123
Kean, Betty and Jane, 144
Keaton, Buster, 87
Keeler, Ruby, 80
Keith and Albie circuit, 123
Keith-Albie combine, 87
Kendall, Messmore, 118

Kern, Jerome, 67
King and I, The, 98
King Kong, 76
Kinsey sign, 98
Klaw, Marc, 87
Klaw/Erlanger Theater Syndicate, 28
Kleenex tissues sign, 99
Klein, George, 161
Klein, Julius, 72
Knickerbocker Hotel, 15, 48, 52, 152
Koch, Edward, 155, 161
Konica sign, 156
Kools sign, 72

L

La Guardia, Fiorello, 63, 88, 97, 106
Lady in the Dark, 98
Laff Movie Theater, 165
Lamb, Thomas, 117, 165
Lamb's Club, the, 8
Lansky, 64
"Last fling" syndrome, 106
Latin Quarter, 124
Lee, Gypsy Rose, 88
Legs Diamond, 64
Leigh, Douglas, 72, 99, 131, 151, 156
Lemidoff, Leon, 76
Lerner, Alan Jay, 98
Liberty Theater, 28, 117
Library, New York Public. *See* New York Public Library.
Lindy, the, 106
Lindy's Restaurant, 146
Lippman, Walter, 76
Liszt's Second Hungarian Rhapsody, 117
Livant Corporation, 162
Loesser, Frank, 98
Loew, Marcus, 117, 118
Loewe, Frederick, 98
Loew's State Theater, 118, 120, 149
Long Day's Journey Into Night, 98
Longacre Square, 2, 3, 7, 9, 15, 51, 71
  migration of theater district to, 27–28
  relocation of *The New York Times* to, 19
  renaming of, 7, 9
  See also Times Square.
Luciano, 64
Luna Park, 33
Luxor Hotel, 91
Lyceum Theater, 28, 35, 36
Lyric Theater, 27, 28, 117

M

Macklowe hotel, 156
Macy's sign, 72

Madame Tussaud's Wax Museum, 52, 162
Madden, Owney, 64
Madison Square, 3, 27, 71
Madison Square Garden, 129
Madonna, 80
Majestic Theater, 35
Manhattan. *See* New York City.
Manhattan Plaza, 155
Manship, Paul, 75
Mark, Mitchell, 117
Mark, Moe, 117
Mark Hellinger Theatre, 144
Marriott Corporation, 156
Marriott Hotel, 118, 161
Marriott Marquis, 156
Martin Beck Theatre, 168
Martin and Lewis, 69, 118
Maxim's restaurant, 52
Maxine Elliott's Theatre, 30, 83
Maxwell House sign, 72
Maytag sign, 72
McClellan, Mayor George, 7, 19
McElfratich, J. B., 27
Merchant Seaman's Club, 111
Metropole Café, 52
Metropolitan Opera House, 4, 12, 27, 48, 75
MGM, 118
Midnight Cowboy, 148
Midnight Frolics, 67
Millennium hotel, 156
Miller, Arthur, 98
Miller, Marilyn, 67
"Minnesota Strip, The," 148
Minolta sign, 156
Minskoff Building, 147
Minsky, Billy, 88
Minsky's New Winter Garden Theater, 88
Miss Heatherbloom Petticoats sign, 21, 71
Miss Liberty, 103, 106
Mitsubishi Corporation, 75
Model T Ford, 16
Moore, Grace, 105
Moss, Paul, 88
Motion pictures, 117–118
Motogram "zipper," 20, 106
MTV, 162
Mumford, Lewis, 76
Murray's Roman Gardens, 8, 52, 58, 63, 147
Muschenheim brothers (Ferdinand and William), 45, 48
Muses mural, 165
Music Hall, 64

N

Nagasaki, 106

NASDAQ sign, 162
National Industrial Recovery Board, 88
NBC's Blue Network, 118
Nesbitt, Evelyn, 87
New Amsterdam Theater, 28, 67, 162
New Year's Eve celebration, Times Square, 19–20
New York City
  allure of, 1
  dining in, 8
  expansion of, 2–3
  information center, 135
  theater district of, 27–28, 62
New York Herald, 19
New York Police Department (NYPD), 147, 148
New York Public Library, 41, 44, 134
  views from, north and west, 43
New York Riding Club, 51
New York Theater, 26, 27
New York Times, The, 3, 7, 19, 20, 72, 151, 168
New York to Paris Auto Race, 16, 48
New Yorker, 72
Newsday, 147
"Newspaper row," 3, 19
Ninth Avenue Elevated Line, 4
Normandy Hotel, 71
Norton, John, 2

Ochs, Adolph, 7, 19, 20, 28, 97, 106, 167
Office of Midtown Planning, 155
Oklahoma, 98
"Old King Cole" mural (Parrish), 48
Olympia complex, 7, 9, 26, 27, 51, 52, 87, 118
One Times Square, 20, 151
O'Neill, Eugene, 98

Pabst Brewery, 4
Pabst Hotel, 4, 5, 7, 19
Palace Beach, 88, 109
Palace Theater, 87, 88, 89, 98, 123, 161
Parade for return of American Expeditionary Forces, 57
Paradise Cabaret Restaurant, 64, 89
Paradise Girls, 89
Paramount Building, 55, 69, 125
Paramount Hotel, 93
Paramount Pictures theaters, 119
Paramount Theater, 105, 118
Parker, Alexander, 151
Parrish, Maxwell, 48
Passing Show, 85

Patience and Fortitude, 44, 134. *See also* New York Public Library.
Pearl Harbor, 97, 105
Pennsylvania Station, 4, 52, 156
Pepsi-Cola sign, 99, 137
PMCs. *See* Private Mailing Cards.
Porgy and Bess, 98
Port Authority Bus Terminal, 140, 148
Porter, Cole, 98
Portman, John, 156
Postcards in America, history of, 5–6
Private Mailing Act of May 19, 1898, 6
Private Mailing Cards, 6
Prohibition, effects of, 8, 48, 51, 52, 58, 63–64
"Prometheus" (Manship), 75
Proskauer Rose law firm, 161
Prudential, 161, 162
Pussy Cat Lounge, 155
Putnam Building, 55, 71

Radio City Music Hall, 75, 76, 77, 113, 118
Rainbow Room, 75
Rapp and Rapp, 69
RCA Building, 75
Recruiting Station, Armed Forces, 106
Rector, Charles, 8
Rector, George, 8, 52, 54
Rector's restaurant, 8, 51, 53, 54, 55
Renaissance Hotel, 156, 161
Republic Theater, 28, 88
Reuters Building, 162
Rialto Theater, 87, 117, 118, 119, 147, 161
Rio Rita, 67
Ripley Believe It or Not Odditorium, 125, 147
Rivoli Theater, 117, 118, 119
RKO Palace Theater. *See* Palace Theater.
Rockefeller, John D., Jr., 75, 76
Rockefeller Center, 75, 76
  Christmas tree, 141
Rockettes, the, 76, 77, 115, 141
Rodgers, Richard, 98
Rodgers and Hammerstein, 98
Rogers, Will, 63, 87
Roman Gardens, Murray's. *See* Murray's Roman Gardens.
Roosevelt, President Franklin Delano, 106
Rose, Billy, 64
Roseland, 80
Rothafel, Samuel Lionel "Roxy," 76, 117, 118
Rothstein, Arthur, 64
Roxy Theater, 73, 105, 118, 121, 126

Roxyettes, the, 118
Rudin Group, 162
Ruppert Beer sign, 98
Russel, Lillian, 8, 54

S

St. Regis Hotel, 48
Sandor the Great, 67
Sanyo sign, 156
Sardi's restaurant, 145
Scandals, 67, 85
Schenley's sign, 98
Seiko sign, 156
Separate Tables, 143
Servicemen postcard (c. 1943), 101
"Sex shops," 148
Sexual revolution, 147
Shanley, Thomas, 52
Shanley's restaurant, 8, 55
Sherry, Louis, 51
Sherry's restaurant, 8, 44, 51, 52, 63
Sherwood, Robert E., 84
Shooting Stars, The, 87
Showboat, 63, 67
Shubert brothers, 64, 67
Shumlin, Herman, 83
"Sign of the Green Dolphin," 51
Simon, Neil, 98
"Sin Street," 147, 148, 152, 162. *See also* 42nd Street.
Sinatra, Frank, 69, 105, 118
Sixth Avenue Elevated Line, 4
Sketch Books, 67, 85
Smith, Kate, 88
Smith, Moe, 63
Sofitel Hotel, 156
Sondheim, Stephen, 98
Sonora Phonographs sign, 72
SONY sign, 156
Sound of Music, The, 98
South Pacific, 98
Souvenir Cards. *See* Private Mailing Cards.
"Speakeasy" establishments, 63, 80
Special Midtown Zoning District, 156
Spectacular Communications, 69
Squibb sign, 72
Stage Door Canteen, 80, 101, 106
Stanley, Morgan, 161
Statue of Liberty at Times Square. *See* Miss Liberty.
Stokes, W.E.D., 87
Strand Theater, 3, 72, 105, 117, 118, 161
Street Car Named Desire, A, 98
"Street of Dreams," 153
Stuyvesant Theater, 30
Styne, Jule, 98
Subway system, 4, 13, 14, 20
Sullivan, Ed, 137
"Sunshine Boys" Smith and Dale, 98

Suzy-Q, 106
Swanee Review, 88
Syndicate, the, 87

T

Tammany Hall, 88
Tandy, Jessica, 98
Taxi dancers, 80
Taylor, Laurette, 35
"Temple of the Motion Picture, The," 117
Theater
in 1940s and 1950s, 97–98, 105
in 1970s, 155
in 1990s, 156
Theater district, demolition of theaters in, 156
Theater district, growth of, 27–28, 62
Theater Sub-District Core Area, 156
"30 Rock." *See* RCA Building.
This Is the Army, 98
Thomas Flyer, 16
Time Headquarters, 75
Times Square
allure of, 1, 2, 8, 167–168
decline of, 147–148
eastern edge of, 44
hotels of, 48. *See also* individual hotels.
illumination of, 8, 68, 71–72, 156
migration of theater district to, 27–28
motion pictures at, 117–118
naming of, 7, 9
New Year's Eve celebration at, 19–20
rebuilding of, 155–156, 161–162
restaurants of, 51–52. *See also* individual restaurants.
Statue of Liberty replica in, 103
subway station, 13, 14, 20, 167
Times Square, general postcards
c. 1905, 25
c. 1907, 11
c. 1911, 17
c. 1912, 23
c. 1918, 68
c. 1922, 65
c. 1927, 79
c. 1935, 90
c. 1938, 78, 95
c. 1943, 107
c. 1944, 99
c. 1955, 136
c. 1956, 133
c. 1958, 139
c. 1966, 150
c. 1970, 154
c. 1985, 147, 157, 158, 159
c. 1994, 160

Times Tower, 8, 9, 19, 20, 37, 39, 50, 52, 69, 106, 135, 147, 150, 152
Times zipper. *See* Motogram "zipper."
TKTS booth, 160, 164
Tobacco Road, 97
Toffenetti Restaurant, 98, 127
Tommy Tucker Band, 105
Traffic signals, automated, 44
Traffic tower, 44, 79
Transportation
- "Broadway Battleships," 28
- elevated railway lines, 4
- horse-drawn vehicles, banning of, 44
- subway system, 4, 13, 14, 20
- Times Square subway station, 13, 20, 167
- trolley service, 65
- vintage coach, 25

Tribune, 3
Trimble Whiskey sign, 71
Trinity Church, 19
Trolley service, 65
Tucker, Sophie, 88
Tweed Ring, 19

U

Union Square, 3, 27
United States Post Office, 5
Upper Broadway, 17
Urban, Joseph, 67
USO, 101, 106

V

Vallee, Rudy, 81
Van Wagner Company, 156
Vanderbilt, William K., 2
Vanities, 67
Vaudeville, 87–88
V-E Day, 106
Victoria Theater, 7, 27, 28, 29, 52, 87, 117, 118, 123, 149, 156
Virgin Corporation, 156
Vitagraph Studio films, 117
V-J Day, 106
Volstead Act, 64

W

Wagner, Robert, 147
Walker, Jimmy, 63
Wallendas, the, 76
Walters, Barbara, 124
Walters, Lew, 124
War Against Pornography, 156
War Mobilization Board, 106
Warner Brothers, 156
Warner Theater, 118
Weber and Fields, 87
Weber and Fields' Music Hall, 3
White, Stanford, 51, 87

White Rock Table Water sign, 71
White Way, 3, 27. *See also* Gay White Way; Great White Way.
Williams, Tennessee, 98
Wilson, Meredith, 98
Winter Garden Theater, 2, 28, 32
Wonderland, 39
Woods, Albert, 165
Woodstock Hotel, 50
World War I, effects of, 6, 8, 63
World War II, effects of, 19, 80, 88, 97–98, 103, 105–106, 124
World's Fair in New York, 88
Wrigley's Spearmint Gum sign, 67, 70, 71

Y

Yacht Club, the, 8

Z

Ziegfeld, Florenz, 67
Ziegfeld Follies, 28, 63, 67, 85
Ziegfeld Theater, 67

About Square One's "Postcards" Series

POSTCARDS FROM. . .

Imagine holding a group of postcards in your hand. Each—through an image and a personal note—captures a moment frozen in time.

The first postcard is dated 1918. A soldier, just returned from the Great War, has visited the New York City Aquarium on the tip of Manhattan. He writes to tell his sweetheart about the excitement of the big city. On another card, an Iowa businessman tells his wife and children that he has never seen anything quite like the 1933 Chicago World's Fair. On yet another is the thoughtful message of a grandmother informing her children that on October 14, 1949 at 5:35 PM, she arrived safely at her destination, the lovely Raleigh Hotel in Miami Beach.

Now imagine that you hold a book of beautiful postcards. All embrace a common theme, but they span a complete century. Now your hand holds more than a few moments in time. It holds a story told in words and images.

Postcards From . . . is a unique series that tells the story of extraordinary places, times, and traditions through postcards sent by real people. Throughout each book, fascinating text weaves the cards together and offers insights into another place, another time. Whether you are an avid postcard collector or you simply want a fresh perspective on a favorite subject, you are sure to find *Postcards From . . .* a true delight.

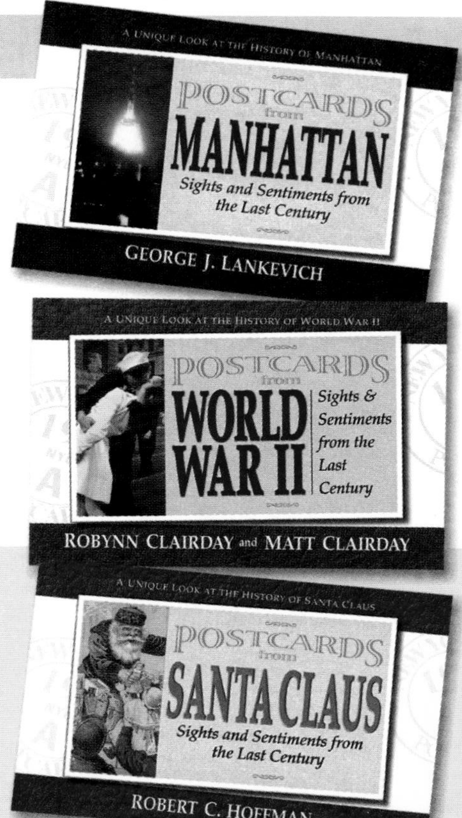

POSTCARDS FROM MANHATTAN

George J. Lankevich

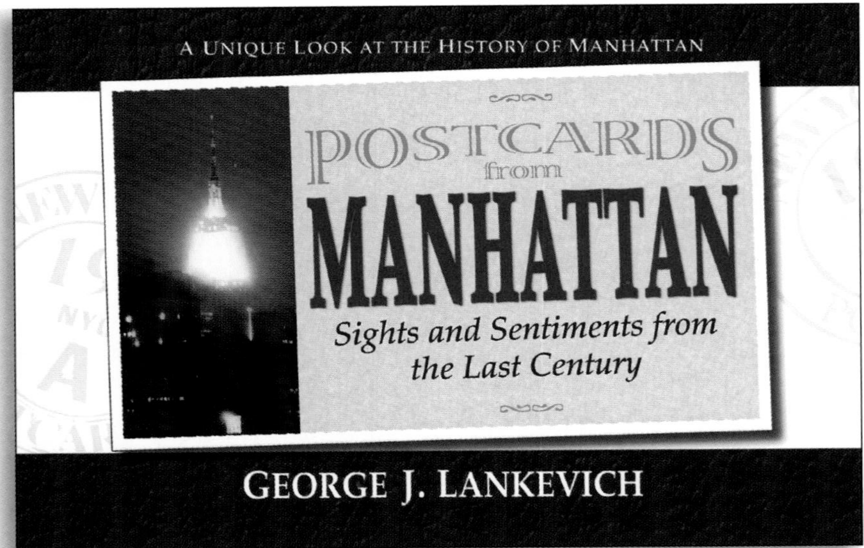

Though known for its enduring landmarks, New York City has experienced sweeping changes over the years. It's seen buildings rise and fall; fashions come and go; and neighborhoods flourish, fade, and reinvent themselves.

Through postcard images and messages, *Postcards From Manhattan* takes you on a guided tour of New York old and new. Arranged by region, 120 beautiful postcards show the evolution of seven distinct areas of the city: the tip of Manhattan, lower Manhattan, midtown Manhattan, upper Manhattan, Central Park, the East Side, and the West Side. You'll visit lost New York, where magnificent hotels like the Astor pampered the rich and famous. You'll see the changing face of landmarks like Pennsylvania Station and Madison Square Garden. And you'll view sights that continue to attract visitors today—the towering Empire State building, legendary Tavern on the Green, and beautiful Central Park.

Postcards From Manhattan offers a unique view of a city that has changed with the times, while retaining its distinctive style and spirit. Throughout, you'll learn how the city that never sleeps has attracted, captivated, and mesmerized New Yorkers and visitors alike—year after year, decade after decade.

$14.95 • 192 pages • 8.5 x 5.5-inch paperback • Full Color • ISBN 0-7570-0101-7

POSTCARDS FROM WORLD WAR II

Robynn Clairday and Matt Clairday

For Americans, the war changed everything. Sons and daughters were separated from their parents; husbands, from their wives. People who had never travelled more than fifty miles outside their towns, found themselves thousands of miles from home. For those who lived through this time, the memories run deep. For those born after this period, their picture of the war is shaped by movies and books. *Postcards From World War II* is a unique look at this history of our nation presented through postcard images and messages.

Here, in this beautiful full-color book, are over 100 actual postcards that reflect a host of scenes, situations, and emotions. Chronologically arranged—beginning with 1941 and ending with VJ Day—the book takes us from the training camps of the South to the battle grounds of Africa, Europe, and Japan; from furlough in New York City to sweethearts at home. Included are fascinating insets that highlight aspects of the time, including the importance of the USO, censorship of letters, women at work, and so much more.

Throughout World War II, postcards provided a wonderful way for those on the home front to stay in touch with those on the battlefront. *Postcards From World War II* offers a glimpse of that extraordinary time.

$14.95 • 192 pages • 8.5 x 5.5-inch paperback • Full Color • ISBN 0-7570-0102-5

POSTCARDS FROM SANTA CLAUS

Robert C. Hoffman

For well over 150 years, the imaginative illustrations of Santa Claus, alias Kris Kringle and Old Saint Nicholas, have amused adults and delighted little children the world over. Since he first appeared in the nineteenth century, his image has been ever-evolving—from that of a thin woodsman dressed in green to that of the jovial rotund figure we know today.

In *Postcards From Santa Claus,* author Robert C. Hoffman presents a collection of over one hundred beautifully colored picture postcards that trace the development of Santa throughout the last century. From the turn-of-the-century Santa to the Santa of the roaring twenties to the Baby Boomer Santa, we experience a unique visual history of this Christmas icon. In addition to pictures, the book shares with its readers personal messages of love, well wishes, and joy—frozen in time. Throughout are insets that highlight fascinating Santa trivia such as the origin of the Santa legend; the creator of the Santa we see today; Santa's names around the world, and much more.

For those who love the spirit of Christmas, *Postcards From Santa Claus* can evoke wonderful holiday memories all year round.

$14.95 • 192 pages • 8.5 x 5.5-inch paperback • Full Color• ISBN 0-7570-0105-X

Rectors
GRILL
Rectors
BALL
ROOM
de
LUXE
Rectors

French-trained chef George Rector offered opulent surroundings, excellent cuisine, and discreet gambling facilities to patrons like Lillian Russell and "Diamond Jim" Brady. [c.1915]

The Putnam Building, on 43rd Street and Seventh Avenue, held Shanley's "lobster palace" restaurant, Rector's cross-Broadway rival. The site was later razed to construct the Paramount Building. [c.1918]

POST CARD.

THIS SPACE FOR COMMUNICATION. ADDRESS

U.S. POSTAGE 1 CENT 1

U.S. POSTAGE 1 CENT 1

NEW YORK, N.Y. MAR 25 7 PM 1919 WASHINGTON BRIDGE STA.

We have been having a fine time. Saw the parade to-day. 26 000 men in line marching four hours. The day is perfect. Eunice & Miriam join me in greeting to you all — M. K. Ross

Mrs J. V. Shearer,
East Sherman St nr.
Morton,
Germantown,
Philada,
Pa.

Parades have always been a joyous part of the New York experience. Here, Fifth Avenue crowds celebrate the return of the American Expeditionary Forces. Perhaps one of the bystanders was the author of the message on the opposite page. [c.1919]

No Times Square restaurant could match the decor of the "Roman Gardens" Murray built on 42nd Street. Ruined by Prohibition, the site became a flea circus after 1925. [c.1918]

Churchill's overcame the bawdy reputation of its adjacent hotel, and became a beloved and economical Broadway institution. [c.1912]

POST CARD

NEW YORK, N.Y. STA. E
APR 13
6-AM
1912

2

U.S. POSTAGE
1 CENT 1

Fine Table d'hote
$1.00 dinner—
—with 12 Orchestra
Specialists singing—
1000—at tables,
you can sit in
gallery, enjoy
your meal, your
prospects & think
where to go to next.
JC

Mrs Nena Henry Brown
of Carnegie Steel Co.
Charleston
W.Va.

THIS SPACE MAY BE USED FOR MESSAGE

THIS SPACE FOR THE ADDRESS

In 1894, Delmonico's moved north from Madison Square to Fifth Avenue to serve casino patrons, but became a favorite destination for discriminating couples from the entertainment center. [c.1904]

For budget-conscious tourists, nothing in Times Square compared to the variety and quality of Automat food. Nickel coffee outlasted two world wars. [c.1918]

CHAPTER TWO

Between the Wars, 1919–1941

By the end of World War I, Times Square was well established as the entertainment center of New York. It boasted nearly fifty theaters, Manhattan's finest restaurants, and a host of cabarets. Times Square was the center of the "white light" district, but there were undoubtedly adjacent blocks where red lights appeared at night.

The corner of 42nd Street and Broadway was the busiest intersection in the bustling metropolis, and the theater district would offer an average of 200 shows a year during the 1920s. In 1928, the busiest year in theater history, 264 productions played in seventy-six theaters, including the immortal *Showboat.* Times Square continued to thrive although it was forced to cope with two disasters, a ban against the sale of alcohol and the Great Depression. It managed to overcome both and enhanced its reputation as the place to go.

Prohibition went into effect on January 16, 1920, and as legitimate drinking ended, funeral services were held in bars across the nation. But despite the confident pledges of federal enforcement agents—"there will be no violations to speak of"—Times Square experienced no liquor shortage over the next thirteen years. Any thirsty soul could buy any drink he wished at a moderate price. At the *Follies,* humorist Will Rogers told audiences that "the worst crime a child could commit was to eat the raisins Dad brought home for fermenting," but visitors to Times Square had no problem finding better brews. The real victims of Prohibition were fine restaurants whose profit margins were determined by liquor sales. Because of the Eighteenth Amendment, famed culinary institutions such as Sherry's (1919), Delmonico's (1923), and Murray's (1924) were forced to close, and boisterous roof gardens ceased to function. In their place, New York had the "speakeasy" on the side street—an estimated 5,000 by 1922, and an amazing 30,000 by 1929. Hundreds of these illegal establishments operated in the Times Square area, and lively nightlife thrived despite periodic efforts by law enforcement agencies. Not surprisingly, "supercops" Izzy (Einstein) and Moe (Smith)—who were responsible for 20 percent of all liquor arrests and the confiscation of 5 million bottles of booze—were let go "for the good of the service" in 1925. When both Fiorello La Guardia and Clarence Darrow condemned Prohibition as "unenforceable bad law," New Yorkers cheered. After 1925, "night mayor" Jimmy Walker ended all attempts to enforce the Volstead Act, and Times Square became the wettest spot in the city.

The paradox of Prohibition was that it financially punished those businesses that obeyed the law. The result was the most uninhibited period of Times Square history, as racketeers and bootleggers boldly walked the streets of the district. The Broadway Mob—Adonis, Costello, Lansky, Luciano, and Siegel—controlled liquor sales; while hoodlums like Legs Diamond, Larry Fay, "Waxy" Gordon, and Owney Madden operated nightclubs. Violence was always just beneath the surface, as the 1928 murder of Arthur Rothstein, the 1929 shoot-out at the Hotsy Totsy Club, and the 1930 disappearance of Judge Crater illustrated, but it only seemed to draw more customers. Billy Rose suggested that Broadway was the only place hoodlums were welcome.

The Crash of October 1929 and the formal end of Prohibition in 1933 brought this gaudy period of Times Square history to a close. The era of hoodlums, flappers, jazz, and booze ended, but Times Square still had to make a dollar. Moreover, the Depression virtually destroyed theatergoing for a few years. The times were changing, and a small group of entrepreneurs suddenly began to create a new version of Times Square.

First among this new breed was Nils Granlund, who broke with his gangland partners in 1930 to offer "family man" entertainment—mass-produced meals and no liquor—at his Hollywood and Paradise Restaurants. His revues continued to feature the ornamented female body, but he packaged it so wholesomely that a man could bring his wife to the show. Volume of business was the key to Granlund's success, and his rival Billy Rose saw opportunity in the many theaters left empty by the Depression. In 1934, Rose converted a silent stage into the Casino de Paree, quickly following that club with the Music Hall and then the Casa Manana in the Earl Carroll Theater. His greatest achievement was the Diamond Horseshoe, a theater-restaurant with "Gay Nineties" decor and "new entertainment spectacularly presented." Rose—a showman and impresario, and husband of Fannie Brice—made "tie-in" deals with hotels and concierges, and his "value" package included backstage tours and introductions to showgirls, his "long stemmed roses." Repeal of Prohibition meant that his "guests" could enjoy a four-course dinner, a drink, and a show for $2.50. By the 1940s, the Diamond Horseshoe alone was grossing a million dollars annually. But the single largest, though not the most profitable of the dinner theaters, was Joe Moss's International Casino on 45th Street, whose 250-foot sign ushered visitors into a modernistic wonder of technology. The International offered Las Vegas glitter before there was a Las Vegas.

Times Square changed radically between the wars, becoming less elitist and more democratic. But it is also fair to say that it lost a bit of its glamour in the process. No longer were theaters on the main avenues, for economics had forced them onto the side streets. Ziegfeld was dead, but the Shubert brothers kept Broadway afloat through its darkest period. Movie palaces offering multiple daily shows replaced both the legitimate stage and vaudeville as the primary entertainment experience, and after 1927, they offered "talkies" as well. Perhaps most sad was the decline of 42nd Street from a dream world of theater greatness to an expanse of "grinder" theaters where movies played continually, and tawdry burlesque houses. In the judgment of some critics, flash had given way to trash.

In 1922, Times Square featured many electric signs and an underutilized north tower, but traffic still seemed manageable. Trolley service lasted until 1946. [c.1922]

TIMES SQUARE, NEW YORK CITY

Times Square is formed by the intersection of Seventh Avenue and Broadway at 42nd Street. It is the very heart of the New York theatrical district, this part of Broadway being known as "The Great White Way."

R-43737

POST CARD

THIS SPACE FOR WRITING

THIS SIDE IS FOR THE ADDRESS

PUBLISHED BY AMERICAN ART PUBLISHING CO.

H. FINKELSTEIN & SON

21

Dear Ralph:
At last, after a day on the train, we have arrived at the "big city." We are staying at Hotel Grand. We will leave tomorrow morning for Washington where we plan to stay a few days. Will arrive at Dugger about next Tuesday night. We are seeing famous places every hour now. As I look out of my window I can see billions of dollars worth of buildings. I will write you more a little later.

Charles G. Neal.

Snowing a little today.

Mr. Ralph Case,
481 St. John St.,
Portland,
Maine.

The Great Ziegfeld

If any name conjures up the image of lavish theater entertainment, it is Florenz Ziegfeld (1867–1932), the man who brought the *Follies* to Broadway. Born in Chicago, Ziegfeld first arrived in New York during the 1890s as the manager of Sandor the Great. On a European tour, he discovered Anna Held, and brought her to the metropolis in 1896. Held became Ziegfeld's wife, appeared in seven of his productions, and became Times Square's first musical comedy star. She also provided Ziegfeld with the idea that became the *Follies of 1907.* In partnership with Abraham Erlanger, Ziegfeld presented a *revue*—he introduced that spelling to the United States—in the *Jardin de Paris.* Featuring fifty "Anna Held beauties," the production began Ziegfeld's career of "glorifying the American Girl." Irene Dunne, Marion Davies, Billie Dove, and Paulette Goddard were all stars who first appeared as Ziegfeld girls.

Between 1907 and 1931, Ziegfeld produced twenty-one different *Follies,* supplementing them with *Midnight Frolics* held atop the New Amsterdam Theater from 1915 to 1922. During the 1920s, he created two to three shows annually, using Jerome Kern, Irving Berlin, George Gershwin, and Rudolf Friml as his composers, and bringing Marilyn Miller and Eddie Cantor before the public. In February 1927, he opened the magnificent Ziegfeld Theater, designed by Joseph Urban, where he produced *Rio Rita* and the incomparable *Showboat.* Ziegfeld's career featured many financial setbacks, but the Crash wiped him out, and by 1932 he was working for Sam Goldwyn in Hollywood. After Ziegfeld died of pleurisy, his second wife, Billie Burke, presented two additional *Follies* in partnership with Flo's longtime enemies, the Shuberts. The Broadway showgirl in *tableau* is perhaps Ziegfeld's greatest legacy, and the *Vanities, Scandals,* and *Sketch Books* that periodically came to Broadway were all imitations of the master showman.

The "spearmen" in the Wrigley's sign (top left) did their "daily dozen" exercises in full view of Times Square. [c.1922]

For almost a century, the lights of Times Square have provided the grandest free spectacle in America. During the 1920s, neon signs replaced the electric bulb. [c.1918]

The Paramount

Constructed in 1926, the Paramount Building immediately became an icon of Times Square. Rapp and Rapp designed an Art Deco pyramid—culminating in a clock tower and a nineteen-foot globe—which may still be the finest building on the square. Headquarters for a film studio, the Paramount offered a movie theater and Child's Restaurant on Broadway, both famous rendezvous spots. Stage attractions from Frank Sinatra to Harry James, from Martin and Lewis to the Beatles, filled the Paramount's 3,664 seats until it closed in 1965, and its marquee was destroyed. Restored in the 1990s, the structure now provides office space for companies such as Spectacular Communications, which builds many of Times Square's illuminated signs.

After 1926, the pyramid-like ziggurat that tops the Art Deco Paramount Building dominated Times Square. [c.1937]

The second of Wrigley's famous Times Square signs, the "Aquarium" featured a pack of spearmint gum the size of a city bus. [c.1939]

Commercialism and the Great White Way

Paris may be famed as the "city of light," but New York perfected the magnificent ability to use lights as commercial stimuli. Gaslights flickering behind glass caps in perforated metal shields were the rule when the "Gay Nineties" began, but the domination of Edison's incandescent lamps was well established by the end of that decade. The first electric sign had gone up on the side of the Cowcatcher Building in Madison Square in 1892—it advertised Manhattan Beach homes—and theater marquees soon adopted a similar glow. Actress Maxine Elliott was probably the first star to "see her name in lights" at the theater named in her honor. At that time, shows were advertised primarily through billboards, but designers quickly perceived the multiple possibilities of lights and turned their attention to creation of the huge display signs for which Times Square is famous. Within the modern industry, such commercial signs are known as "spectaculars," and after 1900, they became an integral part of the cityscape. Advertising became a critical aspect of the Times Square experience—and remains so to this day.

The advance of electric light advertising was orchestrated by O.J. Gude (1862–1925), the first "lamplighter of Broadway" whose genius created a new field for publicity men. Often given credit for inventing the phrase "Great White Way," Gude dominated Times Square displays for a generation. A significant early creation of his inventive mind was a fifty-foot-high Heinz pickle, which some viewers found indecent. The first electric sign in Times Square itself seems to have been a 1903 ad for Trimble Whiskey that appeared on the building which marked the northern boundary of what was then called Longacre Square. But by 1905, the Trimble ad was joined by light displays praising the wonders of C & G Corsets, CC Ginger Ale, and lingerie worn by Miss Heatherbloom. When the silent movie *Ben Hur* opened in June 1910, the Edward Rice Company created an electric sign depicting a chaotic chariot race. The sign filled the side of the Normandie Hotel on 38th Street and Broadway, and was so intriguing that it could literally stop traffic. As early as 1912, English writer Arnold Bennett marveled at the "enfevered phantasmagoria" of Times Square "sky-signs." The moving signboard, Gude exulted, "Forces its announcement on the vision of the uninterested" and revolutionized advertising. His twenty-four-foot Corticelli Spool Silk kitten (1912) and White Rock Table Water (1915) spectaculars confirmed that electricity had conquered Broadway.

Gude's career reached its peak in 1917, when he unveiled the largest sign yet built for Times Square—a 200-foot spectacular designed for Wrigley's Spearmint Gum, which he placed atop the Putnam Building on the West Side of Seventh Avenue at 43rd Street. A dazzling display boasting 17,500 bulbs, the sign featured peacocks, flowing fountains, and six "spearmen." The electrical sextet performed a series of exercises that New Yorkers labeled "the daily dozen," and they persevered in their duty until 1923. Such spectaculars indicated that profit-stimulating commercial advertisements were entitled to more prominence than any theatrical attraction, and between 1919 and 1922, the number of come-ons in Times Square increased by 600 percent. Once again, an Englishman, Lord Chesterton, expressed reluctant awe. "What a glorious garden of wonders . . . (Times Square) brings to anyone who is lucky enough to be unable to read."

Commercialism and the Great White Way

But even as Chesterton wrote, the world of signage was changing, and during the 1920s, neon lighting gradually replaced the electric bulb. Energy efficient, longer lasting, powerful yet cool, and able to project its glow into the darkest night, neon would add a glorious variety of colors to Times Square. Although French inventor Georges Claude held patents on neon technology that were valid until 1932, his rights hardly mattered to the merchants of hype who served American capitalism. Quickly, a forest of spectaculars sprouted despite a docket of pending court cases. Neon signs for Camel, Squibb, Chevrolet, Maxwell House, Sonora Phonographs, Hoover Typewriters, and Maytag, as well as four separate Macy's ads, were among those demanding the attention of potential customers. No longer did signs have to tell an extended story; they were simply visual stimuli designed to encourage purchases. Even the *Times* joined in the celebration of light by putting its name in thirty-foot letters atop its tower.

The biggest Times Square sign of the 1920s was constructed at the request of Edward Bernays, Gude's successor as ad man of the decade. Bernays believed that it was his job to connect the seller with the buyer, and that for advertisers, Times Square had become the "center of the universe." In 1928, his six-story-high, half-block-long sign advertising Dodge cars on top of the Strand Theater was seen by a million people daily. The huge blue-and-white letters of his spectacular completed the triumph of neon. Assistant Secretary of Commerce Julius Klein told the Broadway Association that "light increases the advertising value" of all products, and that glowing signage was "magnificent." Even the *Times* editorialized that "the white lights celebrated in song and legend are now almost obliterated by the reds, greens and orange-yellows." But not even the brightest colors could overcome the effects of the Depression, and the Dodge Brothers sign was one of the first to close in the wake of the Crash of 1929.

Times Square, like the rest of America, was first shocked, then frightened by the crisis of capitalism, but it rebounded quickly. During the 1930s, a new guru of advertising began to make his reputation in Times Square. Douglas Leigh (1907–1999) placed his first spectacular on Broadway and 47th Street in 1934—an A & P coffee cup that steamed there for years. Leigh would create thirty other signs before 1941, and his brilliant rise as the "Young Man of Manhattan" would make him the subject of a *New Yorker* analysis. Times Square was the arena in which commercial America and artistic America intersected. Bubbling Bromo, penguins smoking Kools, and a clown tossing Ballantine rings were among Leigh's contributions to the fabulous clutter of the area. As the culmination of his efforts, Leigh created the most famous sign in history—a Camel cigarette smoker who in June 1941, began to blow perfect smoke rings from his perch on the façade of the Claridge Hotel. The rings were, of course, steam, but they floated over Times Square crowds for the next twenty-seven years, and the sign was reproduced in twenty-two other American cities. Like Gude and Bernays, Leigh understood that Times Square had become a citadel of consumerism. His efforts helped make the area a "desire site" where the proudest accomplishments of capitalism were on display in full color and glittering lights.

The Roxy Theater, the greatest "movie palace" in Times Square, operated between 1927 and 1961. More than 6,000 people could watch a movie and stage show in air-conditioned comfort. [c.1935]

THIS SPACE FOR WRITING

51

NEW YORK, N.Y.
APR 3
10-PM
1935

POST CARD

THIS SPACE FOR ADDRESS ONLY

UNITED STATES POSTAGE
FRANKLIN
1 CENT 1

Guess where we
are

Harry Bert

MANHATTAN CARD PUB. CO.

MCP

Miss Jean Hartmeier
63 Auburn St.
Paterson
N. J.

Rockefeller Center

Rockefeller Center is the most famous commercial development in American history, a complex of nineteen buildings extending over twenty-two acres in midtown Manhattan. Often called "America's Acropolis," the project was originally intended to serve as home for a relocated Metropolitan Opera House, but the Crash of 1929 shattered that dream. Instead, John D. Rockefeller, Jr. ordered his architects to build a "commercial center as beautiful as possible," but one that could return profits. An army of 75,000 workers, laboring during the Depression, completed the first buildings by 1932, and also instituted the Christmas tree tradition. The annual lighting ceremony of a carefully selected fir is now an occasion shared by the entire country via television. By 1933, the centerpiece of the project—the RCA Building—had opened for business.

At the base of "30 Rock" sits a justly famous sunken plaza. Originally intended only as an entryway to underground shopping, later designers transformed this central area into a summertime restaurant and a winter skating rink. As visitors amble down the sloping Channel Islands between the British and the French Buildings, they are greeted by a spectacular fountain where Paul Manship's "Prometheus" reigns; almost everyone takes a picture. At the top of the renamed General Electric Building is the Rainbow Room, which has been the most elegant of all Manhattan cabarets since 1934.

Ever since the 1940s, Rockefeller Center has been enormously profitable. Today it boasts ten landmark office buildings, including Associated Press and Time Headquarters, as well as Radio City Music Hall. The nation was shocked when the complex was sold to the Mitsubishi Corporation in 1985, but after Japan's "Bubble Economy" burst, the Rockefeller's repurchased it at a bargain price four years later. In December 2000, a real estate consortium purchased Rockefeller Center for $1.85 billion and ended the family connection with the nation's greatest monument to capitalistic enterprise.

After 1933, Prometheus, a huge Christmas tree, and the RCA Building all were integral parts of Rockefeller Center. [c.1937]

Radio City Music Hall

Located at the northwestern edge of Rockefeller Center, Radio City Music Hall cost $8 million to build at the height of the Depression. The joint creation of financier John D. Rockefeller, Jr., designer Donald Deskey, and impresario Samuel "Roxy" Rothafel, the Music Hall paid glorious tribute to Art Deco, and since December 27, 1932 has reigned as the most famous showplace in the nation.

On opening day at the Music Hall, enormous crowds passed through a Grand Foyer—150 feet long and 60 feet high—dominated by mirrors, Lalique chandeliers, and a "Fountain of Youth " mural over the main staircase. Visitors discovered that each of the 5,874 seats had an unobstructed view of the 144-foot-wide stage. Moreover, the men's lounge featured a mural by Stuart Davis, while women could contemplate the "History of Cosmetics" by Witold Gordon. Today's visitors often echo Woody Allen's awed belief that "I was entering heaven."

Beyond visual display, the Music Hall was a marvel of American technology. Thirteen motors lifted a vast curtain towards a gilded ceiling; the stage elevators were so advanced that they were later adapted for aircraft carriers; and the Hall featured the world's most sophisticated lighting system, as well as two Wurlitzer organs. But critics were less than impressed, for the nineteen acts of opening night—including Ray Bolger, the Wallendas, the Corps de Ballet, and the Rockettes—ran very late. Both Walter Lippmann and Lewis Mumford panned the failed operation. Only when the stage shows were shortened, movies were introduced, and the reins of stage management shifted from the hands of the extravagant "Roxy" Rothafel to those of Leon Lemidoff, did their opinion change.

In 1933, the movie *King Kong* was the Music Hall's first big hit, and its first Christmas spectacular appeared that same year, beginning a tradition that continues to this day. A city landmark since 1978, Radio City was brilliantly refurbished in 1999 at a cost of $70 million. The most prominent survivor of the Times Square movie palaces, the Music Hall continues to entertain its devoted fans.

The Music Hall was the scene of impresario "Roxy" Rothafel's last managerial job. [c.1935]

A Depression-era postcard displays the varied attractions of Radio City Music Hall, a New York landmark that for seventy years has given audiences value for money. [c.1936]

Despite fog, rain, and Depression, Times Square retains its glamour and mystique in this evening view. [c.1938]

Until well after mid-century, traffic ran both north and south on Fifth Avenue. Signal towers allowed policemen to direct the never-ending streams of vehicles. [c.1927]

Roseland

Americans love to dance. In Times Square's first generation, the orchestras of fine restaurants and the bands of rooftop gardens set the two-step style, but in the 1920s, the rise of the speakeasy brought about a more uninhibited environment. Dance halls and tango palaces became common, and even during the Depression it was "only ten cents a dance." During World War II, the Stage Door Canteen even invented some of the dances that swept the nation. New dance palaces emphasizing ballroom and specialty dancing continued to open into the eighties.

Since New Year's Eve 1919, the one constant in Times Square's love affair with dancing has been Roseland, the dance palace *extraordinaire.* Created by Louis and Dorothy Brecker, and originally financed by a Pennsylvania brewer, Roseland survived the constant changes in the area and continued as a citadel of terpsichorean delight into the new millennium. Brecker demanded respectful behavior; for sixty years insisted that men wear both jacket and tie; and tolerated no after-hours dating between customers and their paid dance partners, known as *taxi dancers.* But not all of Roseland's patrons had to hire their partners. Roseland devotees in the 1920s included the Astaires and Ray Bolger; Al Jolson met Ruby Keeler on Roseland's dance floor; and in 2000, Madonna could often be found there. Considering its longevity, it is a shock to learn that Roseland did not even obtain a liquor license until the 1950s. Louis and Dorothy Brecker never reconciled themselves to rock 'n' roll, but under new owners in the 1980s there were both male and female dancers ready to take a turn around the dance floor for a fee. Few institutions in Times Square have had such a long and storied history.

RUDY VALLEE ©

PHOTO BY KORMAN

THE ENSEMBLE OF "THE FAMOUS HOLLYWOOD CABARET" RESTAURANT, BROADWAY AT 48TH ST., NEW YORK CITY

Cabaret performances offered patrons a more intimate entertainment experience, and brought them close to stars like Rudy Vallee and his supporting cast. [c.1934]

POST CARD

7254

UNITED STATES POSTAGE 1 CENT 1

NEW YORK, N.Y. OCT 11 10 PM 1934

Miss Margaret Spike.
Freeport.
Maine

MADE IN U.S.A. BY E. C. KROPP CO., MILWAUKEE, WIS.

I am now in a
musical comedy show.
Can you pick me
out?

N. J. Pigott

RUDY VALLEE PHOTO COPYRIGHT BY G. MAILLARD KESSLERE, N. Y.

For many, dramatic theater is the ultimate Times Square experience, and Hellman's 1932 play *The Children's Hour* helped revive the "fabulous invalid" during the Depression. [c.1932]

In 1939, Robert E. Sherwood received one of his four Pulitzer Prizes for *Abe Lincoln in Illinois,* his twelve-scene play showing the emotional development of America's greatest president. [c.1939]

The Broadway showgirl was a fixture of Times Square in the 1920s, whether appearing in the *Ziegfeld Follies*, White's *Scandals*, the Shuberts' *Passing Show*, or the *Sketch Books* and *Vanities* of Earl Carroll. [c.1935]

POST CARD
This Side For Correspondence
TIMES SQ. STA. N.Y.
OCT 26
7 AM
1935
Saw this
instead
Alvin
(This Space For Address)
WASHINGTON
2 CENTS 2
M Miss D. Winthrop
5639 Woodcrest Ave
Phila. Pa

Vaudeville and Burlesque on Broadway

American vaudeville dates back to the 1880s, when theater managers began to offer a series of unrelated acts—magicians, acrobats, singers, dancers, and trained animals—as a single complete bill. Vaudeville proclaimed itself a more "refined" show than the often raunchy skits and minstrel shows that preceded it—more wholesome and even family-oriented entertainment. While this claim was not exactly true, the variety shows did please wider audiences and would find a home on Broadway because of Oscar Hammerstein's vision and mistakes.

Hammerstein's Olympia had never returned a profit, and he lost control of it within three years. Undeterred by grand failure, Hammerstein was already planning to construct the beautiful Victoria Theater on the corner of 42nd Street and Seventh Avenue. He opened it to huzzahs in March 1899, intending to offer drama, musical comedy revues, and variety acts to a public that expected constantly changing presentations. But from the start, Hammerstein was forced to compete with the Syndicate for first-rate talent.

The Syndicate had been created by six booking agencies in 1896, and under the leadership of Marc Klaw and Abraham Erlanger, it prevented Hammerstein from offering the best attractions. It was mortal combat between giants, and the Syndicate intended to destroy their most dangerous competitor. Increasingly, the struggling impresario resorted to vaudeville acts to complete his bills. After his son, Willie Hammerstein, assumed management of the Victoria in 1904, a "high class" vaudeville policy was instituted that filled the theater's 1,250 seats. Willie always tried to present legitimate performers such as Irving Berlin, Weber and Fields, Will Rogers, Fannie Brice, and Buster Keaton, but the unending competition with the Syndicate forced him to create new acts drawn from newspaper headlines. He offered "Conrad and Graham," the murderers of W.E.D. Stokes, as *The Shooting Stars,* while Evelyn Nesbitt, whose affair with Stanford White led to his murder, was *The Girl in the Red Velvet Swing.* He also invited audiences to throw tomatoes at the Cherry Sisters, *America's Worst Act,* and is credited with adding pie throwing to comedy skits. His showmanship allowed the Victoria to net over $20 million in its seventeen-year existence. A quarter of the revenue was sheer profit.

If Willie was intoxicated with vaudeville, Oscar longed to present grand opera and was in an everlasting search for the money to fulfill his dream. The Victoria, now the prime vaudeville location in Times Square, had negotiated exclusive booking rights for certain acts. But to obtain additional funds, Oscar sold these off in the face of Willie's objections. Even before Willie died in 1914, the Victoria had lost its preeminence, and it was soon gutted to become the Rialto Theater, one of the first movie palaces. Vaudeville's center then migrated five blocks northward to gain further glory at the Palace Theater.

Constructed on 47th Street in 1913, the Palace had failed to attract crowds after it opened, but its survival was assured after seventy-year-old Sarah Bernhardt made a guest appearance on its stage. Benefiting from Willie's death, the Keith-Albee combine declared that the Palace would now become the "big time" home of "refined" vaudeville performance. And the claim was true. From prewar times

Vaudeville and Burlesque on Broa

through the 1920s, the Palace was the "Valhalla of Vaudeville," and it was the dream of every act to appear on its stage. Booking agencies filled the Palace and its surrounding office buildings, and the small area across Broadway became known as Palace Beach. Vaudeville acts went from the beach to stages across America. As late as the summer of 1931, Kate Smith set records at the Palace when her *Swanee Review* ran for eleven weeks, but the deepening of the Depression cut the heart out of vaudeville. In November 1932, the Palace began to offer movies exclusively, and with a few brief exceptions, that policy continued beyond World War II. In 1937, when a statue of a beloved local priest was unveiled across the street, even Palace Beach vanished as it became Duffy Square.

As vaudeville began to fade from the New York scene, burlesque—formerly considered the crude and vulgar poor relation of the more proper vaudeville—rapidly filled the entertainment void. Burlesque was far more willing than vaudeville to discard all notions of morals and propriety, and offer unemployed male audiences the full experience of female charm. Its "entertainment" consisted of slapstick sketches, chorus numbers, dirty jokes, and "daring" and "sensational" solo female dances. Unlike vaudeville, its clientele was exclusively male.

Long centered far downtown, primarily at Minsky's New Winter Garden Theater and on Irving Place, burlesque had offered stars such as Fannie Brice, Eddie Cantor, and Sophie Tucker their first stages. But Billy Minsky had invented the runway to bring its other attractions closer to the audience; burlesque did not offer the tame *tableaux* of stationary Broadway nudity, but rather beauty in motion. When Minsky finally arrived on 42nd Street, at the Republic Theater in 1931, burlesque was already "ninety-nine percent strip." The Depression had closed five of the ten legitimate theaters on 42nd Street and the prettiest showgirls were now willing to work for burlesque wages. "Strip tease" gave way to "strip please" as sexy performers like Gypsy Rose Lee were billed over the comics. When the National Industrial Recovery Board regulated workers in 1933, there was even a code to control the number of stripper performances. For three years, Tammany Hall, New York City's dominant political force, did nothing to discourage midtown's discovery of an old art form. It took the unexpected triumph of reformers led by Fiorello La Guardia to close the runways in 1934 and ban the name of Minsky; some offending theaters were closed in 1937. Like vaudeville before it, burlesque died away, although a few strippers found temporary employment on the Midway of the 1939–1940 New York World's Fair. After 1942, Commissioner Paul Moss denied new licenses to all burlesque operators, and 42nd Street theaters were reconverted to all day "grinder" movie houses whose audiences were the poor. Only in retrospect did the 1930s have some benefit for Times Square. Burlesque filled some of its theaters, while economic catastrophe prevented others from being converted into office space. By the end of the decade, 42nd Street evoked only memories of its former elegance, but the structures remained and would flourish once again in the 1990s.

Throughout the 1930s, from vaudeville to family-oriented cabaret, Times Square continued to appeal to mass audiences. [c.1935]

Despite the presence of traffic lights, Times Square seemed the same in 1935 as it had in years past. Note the pyramid atop the 43rd Street headquarters of the *Times*, upper right. [c.1935]

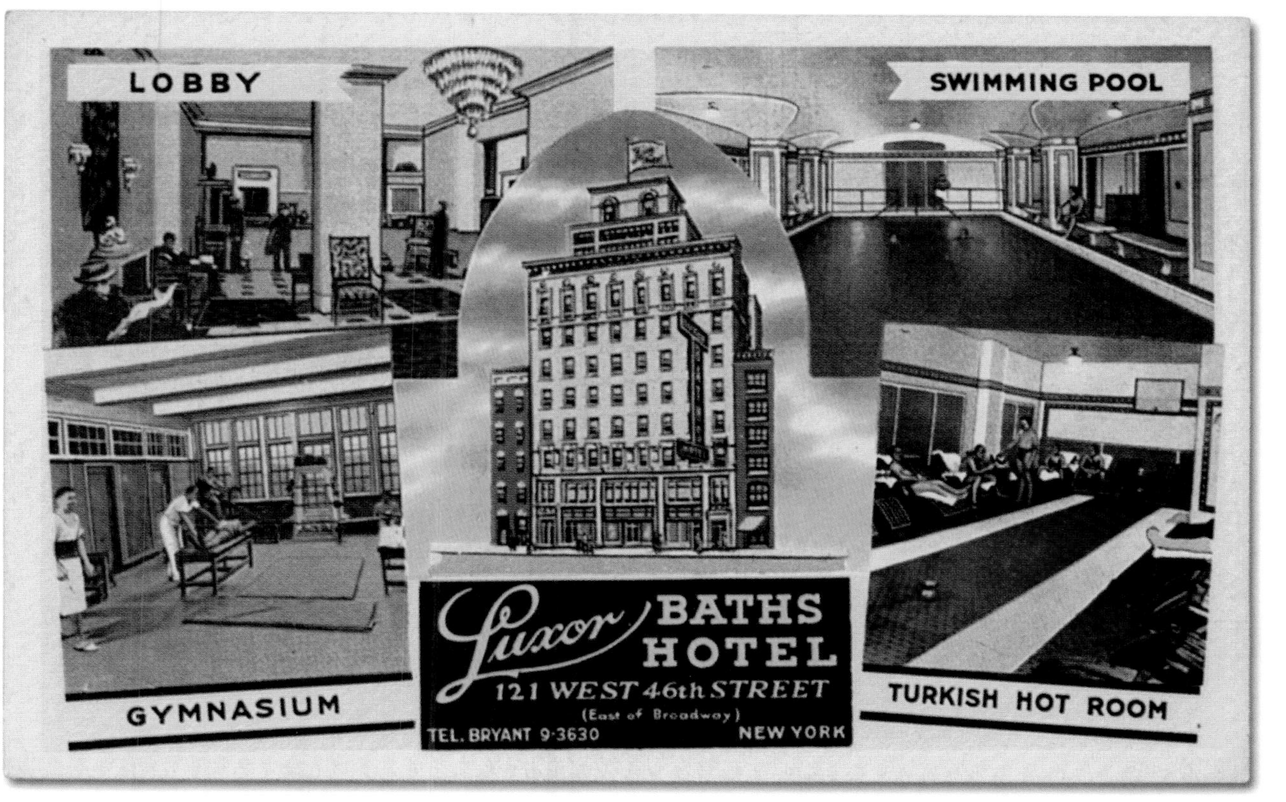

Tourists visiting New York could enjoy every amenity at hotels like the Luxor. [c.1935]

An important part of the Times Square community for over six decades, the Hotel Edison continues to serve tired and hungry visitors. [c.1940]

Times Square's hotels have endured through all area changes, and continue to make it the "most roomed" neighborhood in Manhattan. [c.1932]

HOTEL TIMES SQUARE
43rd Street West of Broadway, New York City
A tower of hospitality in the centre of the centre of New York! Direct subway transportation to the grounds of the New York World's Fair of 1939.

NEW YORK, N.Y.
JUL 30
530PM
1939

POST CARD

BUY U.S. SAVINGS
BONDS
ASK YOUR POSTMASTER

UNITED STATES POSTAGE
GEORGE WASHINGTON 1789-1797
1 CENT 1

PUBLISHED BY RUTH MURRAY MILLER, PUBLISHER, PHILA., PA.

Arrived OK but
a little tired. Going
out to give the Fair
the first glimpse
and get my
bearings. Glad I
made room reservations
as rooms are at a
premium. More later. Jim

Mrs. Margaret Gray
119 Utica St
Ithaca
NY

These skyscrapers appeared on the fringes of Times Square. Not until the nineties would they intrude into the entertainment district. [c.1938]

Page 96: A Times Square landmark, the Horn & Hardart Automat on 46th Street provided coffee, buns, and beans for generations. [c.1938]

AUTOMAT
HORN & HARDART
AUTOMAT
HOT COFFEE
PIES
SECTION OF AUTOMAT MACHINES
Horn & Hardart AUTOMAT — Times Square, New York

CHAPTER THREE

From Triumph to Twilight, 1941–1975

World War II accomplished what Prohibition and economic disaster had been unable to achieve; it turned off the lights in Times Square. In the spring of 1942, military officials ordered the dimming of all lights above street level, and the commercial glories of Times Square went dark. For the next three years, Times Square, like the American nation, devoted all its energy to fighting the fascist enemy. Its confines were to be the scene for many sad good-byes, spirited rallies, and giddy celebrations. In many ways, Adolph Ochs' vision of Times Square as a national town center was fulfilled in the experience of 1941 to 1945.

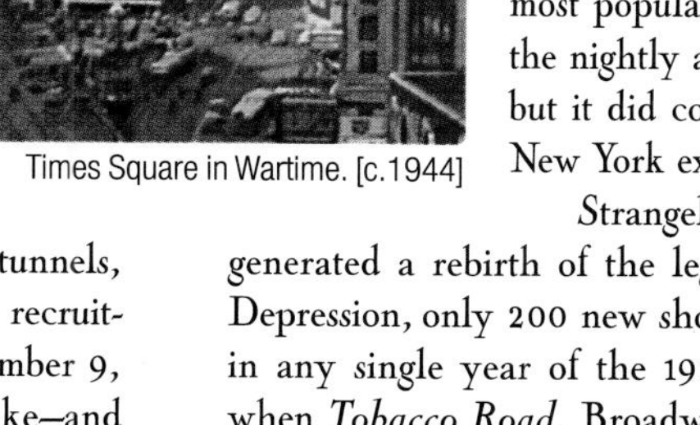

Times Square in Wartime. [c.1944]

After Pearl Harbor, New York City went to war with a will and a fervor that surprised many. Mayor Fiorello La Guardia immediately placed guards at all bridges and tunnels, some 200 Japanese citizens were interned on Ellis Island, and the recruiting stations were overrun with thousands of volunteers. On December 9, 1941, the first air raid alert was sounded—it was, of course, a mistake—and a million school children were sent home early. Engineers soon reported that the subway system was too shallow to provide effective protection against air attack, but as the months passed, it became evident that such dangers were hardly imminent. Instead, the metropolis became a vast staging area for war; half the men and a third of all military supplies went into battle after being shipped from its piers. It was only natural that the concentration of effort and manpower made Times Square into a human beehive, and for the duration of the conflict, it became "the most populated place in the world at night." Not all of the nightly activity was enriching or suitable for all ages, but it did confirm the centrality of Times Square in the New York experience.

Strangely enough, the tragic reality of the war years generated a rebirth of the legitimate theater. During the decade of the Depression, only 200 new shows had been produced, a number exceeded in any single year of the 1920s. Prospects hardly seemed encouraging when *Tobacco Road,* Broadway's then greatest hit, closed in 1942 after a seven-year run. In a year that saw fifty-four shows close, the only hit was Irving Berlin's *This Is the Army,* an all-soldier review that ultimately returned $10 million in revenue to the United States government. But that single success indicated that the Times Square theater audience, increased now by the throngs of wartime, was still available and waiting. The waiting ended in 1943, when Broadway greeted a new form of theater perfected by Richard Rodgers and Oscar Hammerstein II. Drawing lessons from distinguished predecessors like *Showboat* (1927), *Porgy and Bess* (1935), and *Lady in the Dark* (1941), the new collaborators created *Oklahoma* and changed modern musical comedy. *Oklahoma* did not begin with a massed chorus number, offer *tableaux,* or rely on previously heard hit songs. It had a clear plot that integrated original music, athletic dances, and ballet, while its fully developed characters included a villain who died for thwarted love. Rodgers and Hammerstein began a partnership that included *Carousel* (1945), *South Pacific* (1949), *The King and I* (1951), and *The Sound of Music* (1959). They reigned over Broadway even as the ultimate Times Square musical, Frank Loesser's *Guys and Dolls,* opened in November 1950 and ran for 1,200 performances. In their wake came a succession of musical geniuses—Cole Porter, Alan Jay Lerner and Frederick Loewe, Jule Styne, Meredith Wilson, and Stephen Sondheim, to name just a few—who collectively made the next three decades a theatrical golden age. Not that dramatic fare disappeared from the scene. In 1947, Marlon Brando and Jessica Tandy brought Tennessee Williams' *A Streetcar Named Desire* to the stage, and Arthur Miller's *Death of a Salesman* (1949) soon followed. America's most lauded playwright, Eugene O'Neill, offered *The Iceman Cometh* (1946) and *Long Day's Journey Into Night* (1956). On a lighter note, America's most consistently bankable writer, Neil Simon, debuted in 1961 with *Come Blow Your Horn.*

Tally of war bond sales. [c.1943]

Sadly, Broadway's flowering sounded the death knell for vaudeville and burlesque in Times Square. Even the revered Palace resorted to movie presentations, although a 1951 appearance by Judy Garland, backed up by the "Sunshine Boys" Smith and Dale, enjoyed a run of nineteen weeks. Only special concerts by famed entertainers—Betty Hutton (1952), Danny Kaye (1953), and Garland herself—now made money; vaudeville was as passé as the trolleys that no longer ran through Times Square. Huge dinner theaters such as the Diamond Horseshoe, which closed in 1951 after entertaining 4 million guests, were the next to go, quickly followed by most cabarets. In a few years, Times Square changed from the frequent destination of middle-class couples to one used only for a special night out.

After four years of saving, America's pent-up purchasing power was enormous at war's end. Signs directing consumer dollars towards "essential" purchases again proliferated, brighter and more glorious than before. The Camel man continued to smoke, joined in 1946 by a ten-story Budweiser bottle next door, over Toffenetti's Restaurant. Spectaculars for Ruppert Beer, Kinsey, Schenley's, Four Roses, and Johnny Walker also soon appeared. But the most dramatic change came in June 1948, when Dou-

Wartime Times Square was a haven for servicemen, and the postcards they sent home were postage free. [c.1944]

glas Leigh unveiled his 225-foot-long Bond clothing sign, incorporating a 132-inch waterfall and flanked by two seven-story nudes. The waterfall included large amounts of antifreeze to prevent icing over during winter months. These signs were the prelude to the 1950s, generally acknowledged as the finest era of neon art. In 1955, when the Bond spectacular was replaced by Pepsi-Cola, its centerpiece clock became a bottle cap. In the same year, when a charming Little Lulu began to pull Kleenex tissues from her neon box on 43rd Street, the sign had a nationally televised turn-on ceremony. And on Broadway above 49th Street, Automobile Row continued to offer consumers their choice of America's number-one product. Its entertainment mix may have changed by the 1950s, but Times Square still reigned as a corporate "ground zero" designed to stimulate desirable purchasing habits.

In subsequent years, commerce of an entirely different sort gradually drained the luster from Times Square. One by one, the great movie palaces were torn down and replaced by less enticing structures. Neon signs were replaced by individuals offering sex, drugs, or unspecified good times of other types. Times Square entered a period of transition—one that altered its place in the national psyche. For more than half a century, Times Square had drawn everything into its orbit, but now its decline was evident. For the rest of the century, New York would struggle to overcome a generation of decay.

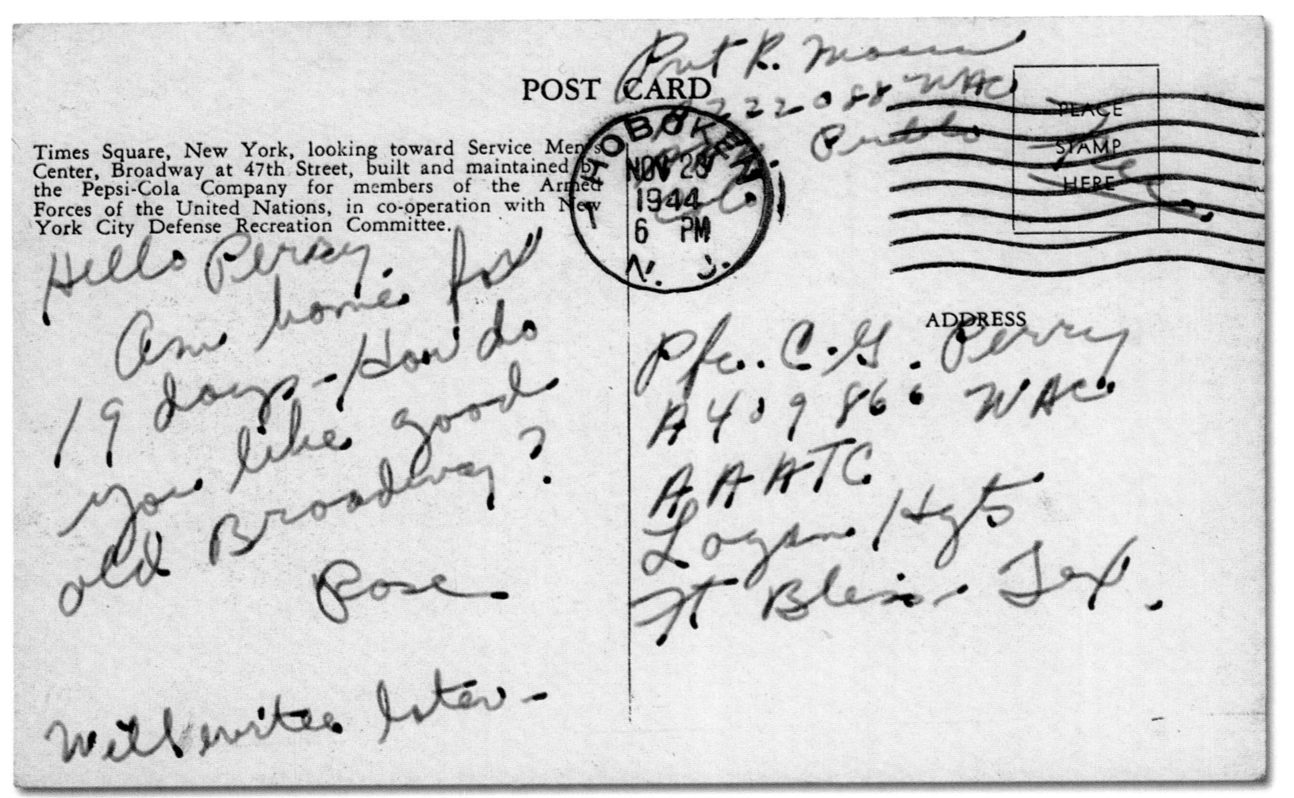
POST CARD

Times Square, New York, looking toward Service Men's Center, Broadway at 47th Street, built and maintained by the Pepsi-Cola Company for members of the Armed Forces of the United Nations, in co-operation with New York City Defense Recreation Committee.

HOBOKEN
NOV 28
1944
6 PM
N. J.

PLACE STAMP HERE

Hello Perry,
Am home for
19 days - How do
you like good
old Broadway?
Rose

Will write later -

ADDRESS

Pfc. C.G. Perry
A409 86 WAC
AAATC
Logan Hgts
Ft Bliss, Tex.

Times Square was "dimmed out" during wartime, but servicemen found food, free show tickets, and companionship at the USO and the Stage Door Canteen. [c.1943]

Millions of servicemen were sent into battle from the port of New York, but Times Square treated them well before they sailed away. [c.1943]

The ever-changing signs at the base of "Miss Liberty" showed the dollar amount of bonds sold at noontime rallies. [c.1943]

Miss Liberty

During World War II, a six-story-high replica of the Statue of Liberty, sponsored by the theater community, presided over Times Square on the traffic island north of 43rd Street. A stage atop Miss Liberty's pedestal drew thousands each noontime for a free show, and provided an occasion for the sale of war bonds. It was later calculated that average daily sales were $60,000, and purchasers got free movie tickets as well. After the war, an army recruiting station was placed where Miss Liberty had stood, and for forty years, it was the most successful post in the nation.

Wednesday 12/13/44

THIS SPACE FOR MESSAGE

Dear Folks. After a Chapter Luncheon at the Inst. for Veterans mailed a package to Jr. P.O. was so crowded at 23rd went down to 11th St. Did some buying at 14th St. then to Times Sqr where we bought a Bond at Statue of Liberty. Big crowd at this rally. People from all over. Machine registered $17,000,000. Your package rec'd yesterday. Thank you. Love Ernie & Lou

P. S. "I bought my bond at the *Statue of Liberty in Times Square."

*ERECTED BY MOTION PICTURES WAR ACTIVITIES COMMITTEE, NEW YORK AREA.

Cold & clear to day.

BRONX CENTRAL ANNEX

NEW YORK N.Y. DEC 14 7 PM 1944

UNITED STATES OF AMERICA
INDUSTRY·AGRICULTURE
FOR DEFENSE
POSTAGE 1 CENT

Mr & Mrs. E. S. Becker
21 Church St
Beverly N. J.

Times Square Goes to War

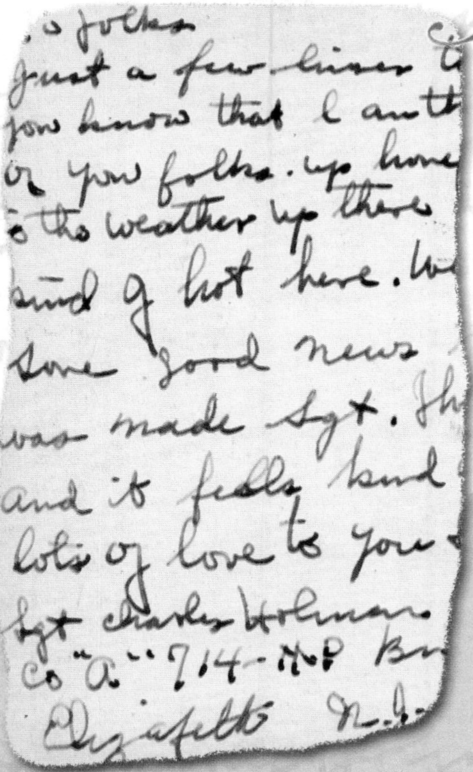
s folks
just a few lines
you know that I am
or you folks. up home
the weather up there
kind of hot here.
some good news
was made Sgt.
and it feels kind
lots of love to you
Sgt Charles Holman
Co "A" 714 - M.P. Bn
Elizabeth N.J.

Mobilizing a nation for war is never easy, but the reaction of Americans to the attack on Pearl Harbor revealed a suddenly united population. In New York City, armed force recruiters were overwhelmed by the response of volunteers. During the terrible winter of 1942, the nation discovered that city lights on shore silhouetted ships and turned them into perfect targets. Doing its part, Times Square dimmed everything above street level, and volunteers saw that the regulation was scrupulously observed. Even if the order had not saved the city a million dollars a year in power costs, public opinion would have enforced the new restriction. War created a more unified and patriotic metropolis, its bravado given voice by Humphrey Bogart in *Casablanca,* the best movie of 1943. In the film, expatriate club owner Rick informs his Nazi opponent that there were sections of New York even the German army would find difficult to enter. In fact, during wartime, Times Square accurately mirrored the patriotic spirit that infused the United States.

Although the Great White Way was dark, Times Square was the primary destination for hundreds of thousands of residents, transients, and servicemen. Crowds filled the streets every evening, and after a dismal theatrical year in 1942, Broadway bounced back with exceptional vigor. Hit shows soon drew enormous crowds, and the great movie palaces did exceptional business by providing stage shows in addition to films. In December 1942, Frank Sinatra first appeared at the Paramount Theater as an "extra added attraction" with the Benny Goodman Band. Although many servicemen resented the fact that "The Voice" had perforated ear drums that kept him out of uniform, Sinatra's triumphant return to the theater in October 1944 set off the Columbus Day bobby-soxer riot. Entertainers did exceptionally well during wartime as showplaces like the Paramount, Strand, Capitol, and Roxy bid for their services. The latter paid $27,000 a week to a bill headed by Danny Kaye and the Tommy Tucker Band, and Grace Moore received $20,000 for her week—this, at a time when the average weekly salary was about $36. When Harry James appeared at the Paramount in 1943, police had to be called to clear the theater of fans who stayed through his show, through the movie *China,* and into the second set. By 1945, stars like Jack Benny, Milton Berle, and Bob Hope commanded over $40,000 a week.

Times Square Goes to Wa

During the war years, servicemen were assured of a friendly reception in Times Square. The USO operated on 43rd Street, where the latest versions of the jitterbug and the Lindy were invented. The Balboa, Jersey Bounce, Jig Walk, Flea Hop, and Susy-Q first appeared there, as did shagging. Free show tickets were almost always available, and afterwards, the Stage Door Canteen on 44th Street provided free food served by Broadway chorus girls and debutantes. There was little sense of Puritanism in wartime Times Square. The nightclub and bar scene was frantic as soldiers and sailors who had money to burn and faced an uncertain future lost all inhibitions. When the War Mobilization Board attempted to order a midnight curfew, Mayor La Guardia extended it to 1:00 AM, and continued to reap the benefits of a 30-percent cabaret tax. A darker side of the "last fling" syndrome was a marked increase in both male and female prostitution.

More than any other American venue, Times Square served as a national town center during the war. The *Times* zipper provided the latest news, cameras recorded the response of citizens, and servicemen filled the streets along with native New Yorkers, visiting war contractors, and bureaucrats from Washington. When President Roosevelt died on April 12, 1945, it seemed natural for crowds to gather around the Statue of Liberty, which still proudly stood on 43rd Street. Shortly thereafter, V-E Day was marked by two celebrations, one premature and the other totally out of control. Like the rest of humanity, Times Square was awed by the atomic weapons that destroyed Hiroshima and Nagasaki early in August 1945. As V-J Day loomed on August 14, huge crowds filled the streets all around the *Times* Tower awaiting word of victory. The police had to close off all traffic, and by 7:03 PM, there were an estimated 750,000 present to read the Motogram announcement, "Official—Truman announces Japanese surrender." By 10:00 PM, over 2 million people were dancing and celebrating, and 5,438 tons of confetti were collecting in the streets. No image captured the thrill of V-J Day victory so well as Alfred Eisenstaedt's photo of a sailor and nurse embracing—naturally, in Times Square.

For a few brief years, Times Square had fulfilled Adolph Ochs' hopes and served as America's civic arena. But in the decades that followed, it lost much of its luster and slid into decay. To the media and the public, 42nd Street between 7th and 8th Avenues was the "worst block" in the city by the 1960s. Yet in one small bit of real estate, the patriotic spirit of the age continued—the Armed Forces Recruiting Station located on the site where the Statue of Liberty once stood. Opened in 1950, the installation was for forty years the most successful recruiting site in the nation, and survived many antiwar demonstrations during the Vietnam years. Dismantled and reconstructed in 1999, it remains active today, a reminder of the time when a totally united America fought the Good War.

Because of wartime gas rationing, Times Square by daylight seemed a bit forlorn, and pedestrian traffic appeared to outnumber the automobiles. [c.1943]

POST CARD
ACTUAL PHOTOGRAPH

NEW YORK, N.Y.
AUG 2?
5 - PM

BUY
WAR SAVINGS
BONDS AND STAMPS

UNITED STATES POSTAGE
GEORGE WASHINGTON
1 CENT 1

A. MAINZER. 18 E. 28TH ST. – NEW YORK, N. Y.

To the gang
This is to all of your
gremlins of Deck 4
who haven't been
out of Brooklyn,
or Deck 4. Here
just spending a
few days in
N.Y. until our
boat sails for
parts unknown.
Love dear
children
Ann & Fran

Brooklyn Public Library
Grand Army Plaza
Brooklyn, N.Y.

"Deck 4"

Father Francis X. Duffy, "Fighting Chaplain" of the 69th Regiment and then pastor of the Holy Cross Church on 42nd Street, presides over what was once the Palace Beach, where vaudeville acts waited for their "big break." [c.1944]

5-29

Dear Mary: Heres N.Y.'s heart - spend most of my time in this section gazing. Stuck my ear in a place + heard Lawrence Welks band for a minute - Count Basie + Phil Spitalny are playing in downtown N.Y. also. Prices here are reasonable. Weather is hot. Sent Roy Reimer a J. Dempsey card. I'll send you my love and the rest I'll save for [illegible]

Bye — Bill

POST CARD

PHOTOGRAPH

STATION

MAY 29 12-M 1944 N.Y.

UNITED STATES POSTAGE

GEORGE WASHINGTON

1 CENT 1

PROD. OF FOTO SEAL CO. - NEW YORK, N.Y.

Mrs Bill McArthur
8316-N. Fessenden (3)
Portland Oregon

Merchant seamen, whose civilian contribution to the war effort was often overlooked, were not forgotten men in Times Square, as shown by this view of the 43rd Street Merchant Seamen's Club. [c.1943]

AMERICAN THEATRE WING
MERCHANT SEAMEN'S CLUB
109 West 43rd Street, New York City
Theatre, Movie, Concert Tickets
LIBRARY - GAME ROOM
Entertainment nightly. Food Bar open from 5 p.m.

BROOKLYN, N.Y. 7
OCT 11
10-PM
1943

POST CARD

WAR SAVINGS
BONDS AND STAMPS

UNITED STATES POSTAGE
GEORGE WASHINGTON 1789-1797
1 CENT 1

On Weekend leave +
strolling around in
N.Y. Just had Eats
in the Seamens Club
+ feel better now.
Letter follows.
Your Cousin Joe

LUMITONE PHOTOPRINT · NEW YORK · MADE IN U.S.A.

Family
Hermann Rebmann
122 Gorton St.
Buffalo N.Y.

AMERICAN THEATRE WING WAR SERVICE, INC.
Stage, Radio, Screen, Vaudeville, Music and all Allied Crafts.

Since opening day, December 27, 1932, Radio City has reigned as the greatest Art Deco theater in the nation, and remains an obligatory tourist destination. [c.1942]

Hi folks
Just a few lines to let
you know that I am thinking
of you folks up home
Is the weather up there
kind of hot here. Well I have
some good news this I
was made Sgt. Thursday
and it feels kind of nice
lots of love to you + yours
Sgt Charles Holman
Co "A" 714 MP Bn
Elizabeth N.J.

NEW YORK, N.Y.
AUG 1
1942

POST CARD
THIS SIDE IS FOR THE ADDRESS

BUY
DEFENSE SAVINGS
BONDS AND STAMPS

PLACE
ONE CENT
STAMP
HERE

Rev. Theador Hayden
1336 1st Ave
Watervliet
N.Y.

MANHATTAN POST CARD PUBLISHING CO., INC., N.Y.C.

MADE IN U.S.A.

The Music Hall Rockettes were not the first dance line to perform in Manhattan's theaters. They merely were the best and the most innovative. [c.1944]

6/16/44

THIS SPACE FOR WRITING MESSAGES E-6798

Dear May - I'm in again - You'd still know there is a war on here. The stores have about the same stuff as at home + sometimes less. We going to see a play tonight - Will write + tell you about it Friday

NEW YORK, N.Y. JUN 16 9:30 PM 1944

Designed and Produced by Harry H. Baumann, 216 W. 18th Street New York, N.Y.

UNITED STATES POSTAGE GEORGE WASHINGTON 1789–1797 1 CENT 1

POST CARD

Miss May Ryder
Smith St
Middleboro
Mass
RFD

Palaces on Times Square

Times Square has always meant excitement and glamour to the American public. It has been the setting for scores, if not hundreds, of Hollywood movies, and people who have never visited New York believe they "know" Times Square because of motion pictures. But few remember that the city gave birth to the film industry, was home to many of the visionaries who created the industry, and hosted innumerable premières. Perhaps above all else, Times Square was the birthplace of the "movie palace"—an almost mythic environment capable of transporting audiences into a fantasy world of sumptuousness and delight. It was Marcus Loew, a motion picture pioneer, who first conceded, "We are selling tickets to theaters, not movies," and then acted to build his own phalanx of palaces. The buildings in which New Yorkers attended movies created a sense of wonder and awe. Using rococo décor, mirrors, and chandeliers, along with Art Deco and Renaissance motifs, they created an atmosphere of luxury and total enjoyment. For decades, the Times Square experience was not complete until visitors fell under the spell of a palace.

The Strand, the first "movies only" theater in Times Square, was constructed in a carriage factory at Broadway and 47th Street by Mitchell and Moe Mark, entrepreneurs of the nickelodeon—the five-cent movie. The Marks hired Thomas Lamb to design the "best" theater on Broadway, and when their 2,800-seat showplace opened on April 11, 1914, it had cost over a million dollars. The Mark brothers' most significant decision was to hire Samuel Lionel Rothafel to manage their palace of "gilt and marble and deep pile rugs." On opening night, Rothafel used four projectors to run the film without interruption, and introduced the evening with Liszt's Second Hungarian Rhapsody played by the house orchestra. In the same year, Hammerstein's original Lyric, renamed the Criterion, began to show Vitagraph Studio films, but the Strand was clearly more elegant in its décor. More important was that *Birth of a Nation,* which played for forty-four consecutive weeks in the Liberty Theater on 42nd Street in 1915, demonstrated to theater owners that movies could be more lucrative than legitimate plays. Before World War I, it was clear that movies and movie palaces formed a dynamic combination.

"Roxy" Rothafel remained at the Strand for only two years because he saw greater opportunity at the corner of 42nd Street and Seventh Avenue. After supervising the gutting of Hammerstein's vacant Victoria, he reopened it in 1916 as the Rialto Theater. Although "The Temple of the Motion Picture" provided platforms for soloists to entertain while reels were changed, film was its primary attraction. It was at the Rialto that "Roxy" first showed the genius for lighting that always distinguished his shows. But shortly after opening, he hired Lamb to design an even more sumptuous setting for the Rivoli, to be built on Broadway and 49th Street. At both theaters, "Roxy's" extravagances were so outrageous that profits were minimal despite many daily shows.

New York executives running Hollywood studios believed it was critical for their films to "open" well in Manhattan. They understood that the economics of palaces were such that few could return great profits; those were garnered on second runs "direct from Broadway." But it was necessary to build showplaces where

Palaces on Times Square

their products could debut. So in 1919, Messmore Kendall converted a livery stable and blacksmith shop on 51st Street into a palace designed to showcase the films of MGM. Poor management forced the closure of the 5,300-seat theater, but Kendall hired "Roxy" to fix the problems, and when the Capitol reopened in June 1920, it became a huge success. Rothafel was the first New York impresario to recognize the potential of radio, and in November 1922, he hosted live shows on NBC's Blue Network. For the next four years, the Capitol and its dynamic manager were the most famous duo in America, drawing thousands of visitors to their palace. Competitors like Loews State (1922), the Paramount (1926), and the Warner (1927) were left in their wake.

By 1926, 96 percent of all American theaters were used to show movies, and palace building had become a major front in studio warfare. In 1927, "Roxy" was pried away from the Capitol by the Fox Corporation, which paid a higher salary, offered stock options, and named a theater in his honor. Located on Seventh Avenue and 50th Street, the Roxy had 5,920 seats; a staff of 300; 100 dancers, including the Roxyettes; and a 100-piece orchestra. Dubbed the "Cathedral of the Motion Picture," it represented the height of elegance in a decade when Americans went to the movies twice a week. Even after the start of the Depression, an evening at the movies provided a luxurious setting in which people could forget their troubles. It is interesting that the greatest of the dream palaces, Radio City Music Hall, opened in December 1932, in the depths of America's economic disaster. And in 1935, when the old Hammerstein Olympia was demolished, the centerpiece of the new block was the Criterion Theater, yet another palace.

In the 1940s and 1950s, the great palaces of Times Square continued to flourish by offering famous entertainers in combination with first-run movies. Big bands, crooners, and acts like Martin and Lewis kept audiences happy—and kept them coming back for more. The world's largest sign stretched for an entire block above the Astor and the Victoria Theaters to advertise motion pictures. Premières at the Criterion meant that traffic was halted and that a red carpet extended across Broadway to the Astor Hotel for first-night audiences. But the slow decline of Times Square and the social revolution that moved America into the suburbs was already eroding palace economics.

The passing of the palaces took almost a generation. The "Cathedral" of the Roxy was first to fall, destroyed in an expansion of the Taft Hotel in 1960. The famous arcade of the Paramount, which had trumpeted the appearances of Goodman and Sinatra and James, was torn down in August 1965. The Rialto closed in 1980, while the Astor and Victoria Theaters were sacrificed to build the Marriott Hotel in the 1980s. The final blow came in 1987, when developers pulled down the Strand/Warner, the Loews State, the Rivoli, and the Capitol. Clearly, an era had come to an end, and many believed that the passing of the palaces meant the end of Times Square itself. But the next decade would show that the entertainment district could overcome even the death of its signature institutions.

The movie palace was a fixture of Times Square for over fifty years. Each Hollywood studio attempted to première its films in the most elegant setting possible. [c.1925]

Loews State was the flagship of Marcus Loew's 1,000-theater empire. [c.1927]

The Roxy used enough power to light a city of a quarter million people. From 1927 to 1961, it was the "Cathedral of the Motion Picture." [c.1951]

WORLD FAMOUS ROXY THEATRE
7th AVE. and 50th St., N. Y. C.

Artist's conception of the Roxy Theatre, showing the exterior view of one of the world's Most Famous Motion Picture Theatres.

17626

A "Colourpicture" Publication, Boston 15, Mass., New York Office, 489 Fifth Avenue

Feb 1, 1951

Hi! Swoon! Swoon!
Just saw Danny Kaye
in Person here!!
Wow! Wonderful.
Movie "Call Me Mister".
Very good. Danny
was better! Your
marks were good!
Study hard & be good.
Love
Mother

NEW YORK FEB 2 '51 N.Y.
U.S. POSTAGE 01
P.B. METER 127637

WRITE MAILING ADDRESS BELOW

Miss Marianne C. Bedell
Residence Hall
Geneseo
N. Y.

Starting in 1949, the Palace offered a mixed bill, but never recaptured the glory of its vaudeville years. [c.1949]

The Palace

Constructed by Martin Beck in 1913, the Palace is probably New York's most famous theater, the home of "wholesome" vaudeville. Yet because of competition from Hammerstein's Victoria, it barely survived its infancy. Taken over by the Keith and Albee circuit, the Palace began to offer a mixed menu of acts in 1914, and soon surpassed the fading Victoria to become the "Valhalla of Vaudeville." Depression economics forced it to show movies, but it returned to a combination program of film and acts in 1950. Subsequently, the Palace served as a concert venue for Judy Garland, Danny Kaye, and Harry Belafonte, among others, and today it is used for legitimate theater performances. Although the interior of the Palace enjoys landmark status, during the 1990s, the exterior was encased by a hotel—first the Embassy Suites, and later the Doubletree Suites.

Club life in Times Square peaked in the prosperous decades after World War II.
The Latin Quarter under Lew Walters, Barbara's father, always provided value for money. [c.1950]

"Believe it or not," Ripley replaced Child's Restaurant at the corner of the Paramount Building. [c.1948]

Large, boxy hotels were needed to house the millions of visitors to Times Square. The Brass Rail restaurant (right) was also a popular tourist destination. [c.1949]

Toffenetti, on the corner of Broadway and 43rd Street, was an after-theater stop famed for its dessert menu. [c.1937]

For a fast protein lift, nothing was better than the Buitoni Spaghetti Bar—not for profit, but for promotion. [c.1950]

Located opposite the third Madison Square Garden, Jack Dempsey's first restaurant was popular with sporting crowds. [c.1936]

The "Manassa Mauler" himself often greeted patrons of his Broadway establishment, which replaced Churchill's as the headquarters for sportsmen of every type. [c.1948]

Douglas Leigh's masterpiece, the 132-foot-long Bond waterfall used twenty-three recirculation pumps and added thousands of gallons of antifreeze during the winter months. [c.1949]

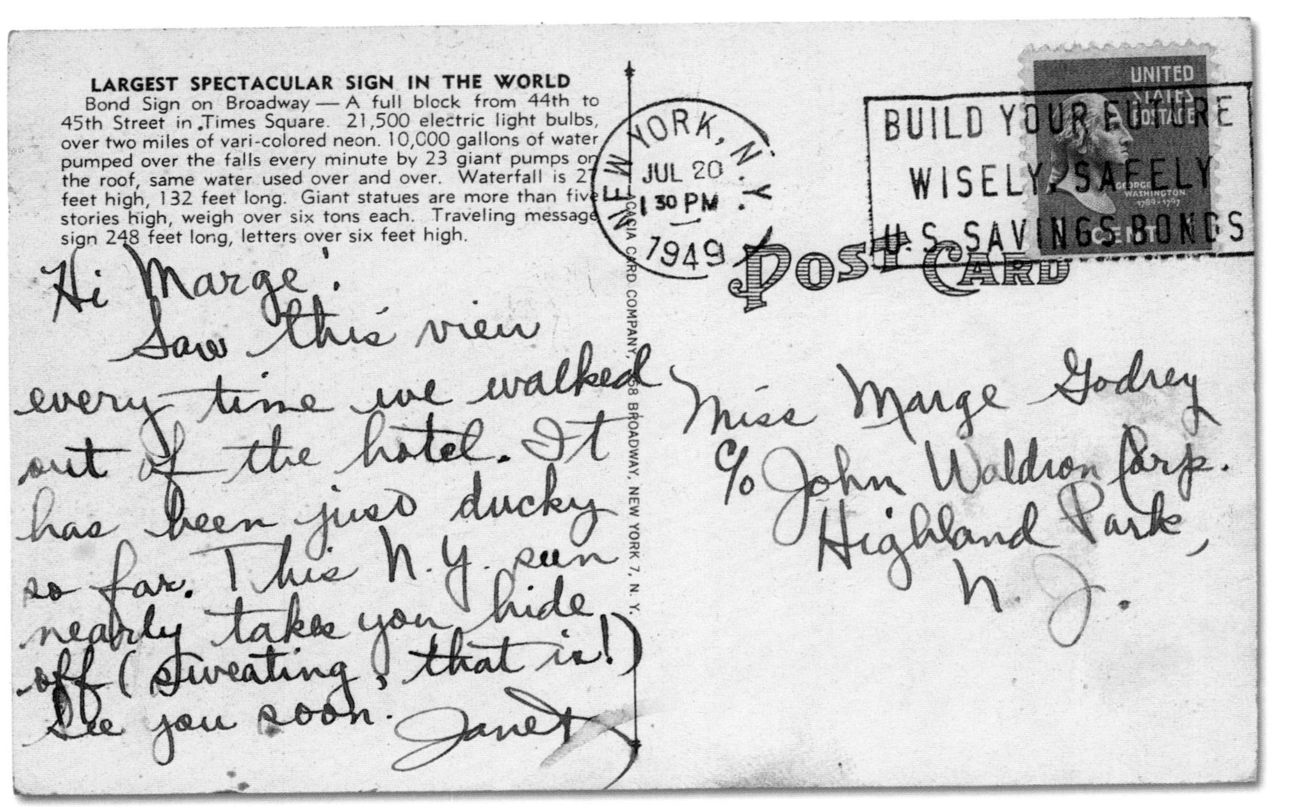
LARGEST SPECTACULAR SIGN IN THE WORLD

Bond Sign on Broadway — A full block from 44th to 45th Street in Times Square. 21,500 electric light bulbs, over two miles of vari-colored neon. 10,000 gallons of water pumped over the falls every minute by 23 giant pumps on the roof, same water used over and over. Waterfall is 27 feet high, 132 feet long. Giant statues are more than five stories high, weigh over six tons each. Traveling message sign 248 feet long, letters over six feet high.

ACACIA CARD COMPANY, 58 BROADWAY, NEW YORK 7, N. Y.

NEW YORK, N.Y. JUL 20 1 30 PM 1949

BUILD YOUR FUTURE WISELY, SAFELY U.S. SAVINGS BONDS

UNITED STATES POSTAGE GEORGE WASHINGTON 1789-1797

POST CARD

Hi Marge!
Saw this view every time we walked out of the hotel. It has been just ducky so far. This N.Y. sun nearly takes you hide off (sweating, that is!) See you soon. Janet

Miss Marge Godrey
c/o John Waldron Corp.
Highland Park,
N. J.

In the 1950s, Times Square traffic ran primarily downtown, and seemed to have won its perpetual battle with walkers. [c.1956]

The New York Public Library's stone lions, Patience and Fortitude, guard the steps and make them one of the most popular viewing sites on Fifth Avenue. [c.1958]

At the base of the *Times* Tower, Hotelings newsstand and the New York City information center offer their services to summer pedestrians. [c.1955]

Commerce and entertainment have always competed for space in Times Square, and probably always will. [c.1955]

By the mid-1950s, Pepsi had replaced Bond atop the waterfall, and Ed Sullivan's face seemed to foreshadow TV's victory over motion pictures. [c.1956]

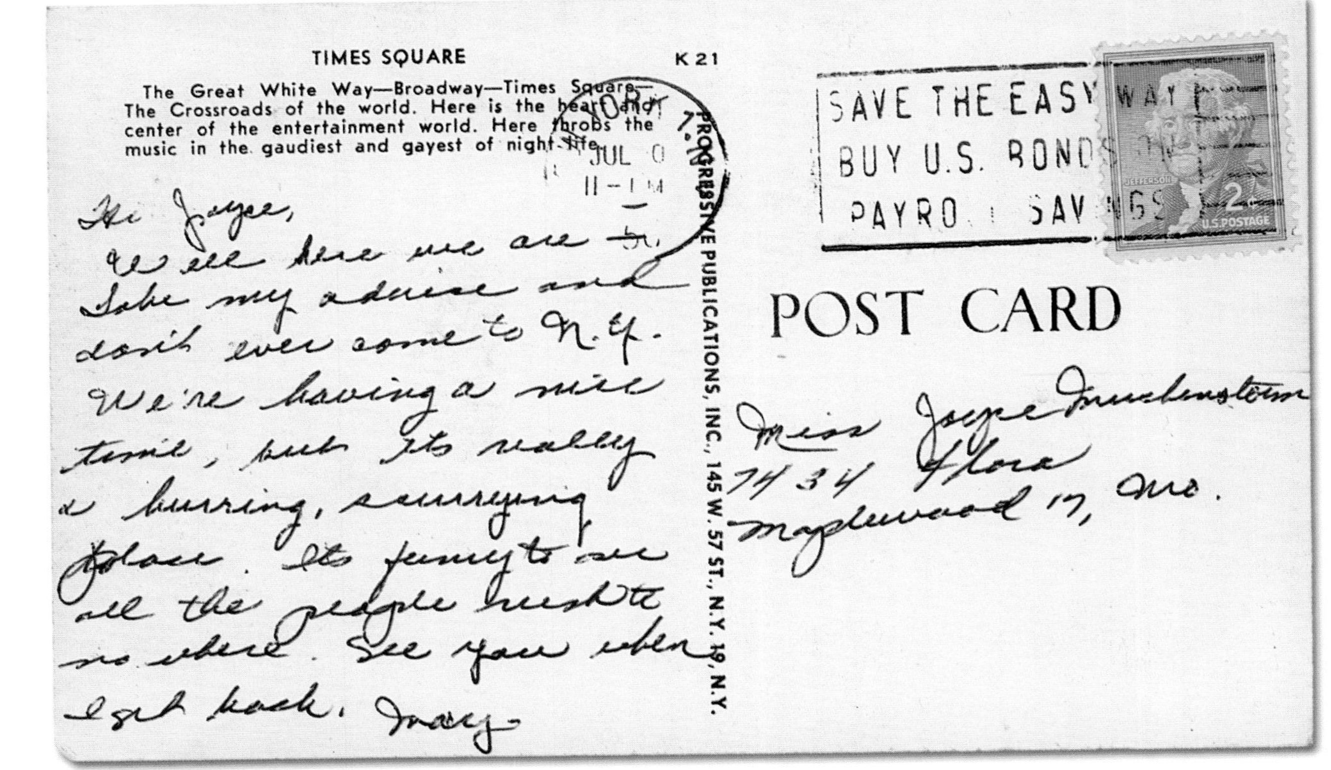

TIMES SQUARE
K 21
The Great White Way—Broadway—Times Square—The Crossroads of the world. Here is the heart and center of the entertainment world. Here throbs the music in the gaudiest and gayest of night-life.
PROGRESSIVE PUBLICATIONS, INC., 145 W. 57 ST., N.Y. 19, N.Y.
SAVE THE EASY WAY
BUY U.S. BONDS
PAYRO SAV NGS
JEFFERSON
2¢
U.S. POSTAGE
POST CARD
Hi Joyce,
Well here we are —
Take my advice and
don't ever come to N.Y.
We're having a nice
time, but it's really
a hurrying, scurrying
place. It's funny to see
all the people rush to
no where. See you when
I get back. Mary
Miss Joyce
7434 Flora
Maplewood 17, Mo.

As the fifties came to a close, Times Square's array of lights hid its slow downward spiral. [c.1958]

Despite several redesigns, the Port Authority Bus Terminal (left) remains a brooding and brutal presence at the west end of 42nd Street. [c.1953]

The Rockefeller Center Christmas tree traces its origins to Depression days, as do the Rockettes. [c.1956]

67 Hudson St. N.Y. 13.

THE ROCKETTES, internationally famed precision dancers, who appear on the world's largest stage at Radio City Music Hall, Rockefeller Center, New York.

NEW YORK 10, N.Y. JAN 24 7:30 AM

MADISON SQUARE STATION

JEFFERSON 2¢ U.S. POSTAGE

POST CARD

Natural Color. Made by Dexter Press, Inc., 274 Madison Ave. N.Y. C.

dear Nellie,

Saw "I'll Cry Tomorrow" at Radio City this pm. Had to write and tell you that the foot warmers were greatly appreciated last week during the Fuel Strike.

Love,

Nellie.

Mrs. Roy Yeungst

302 Parkway Rd.,

Boulevard Park,

Harrisburg,

Penna.

83727

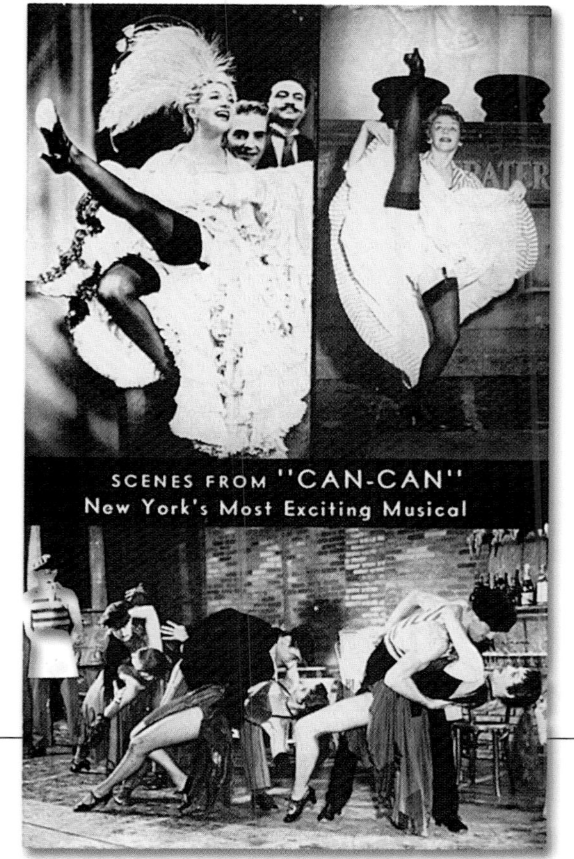

Some critics consider the 1950s to be Broadway's finest decade. Musicals and drama were the staples of the theater district. [c.1953]

Scenes from
"THE FIFTH SEASON"
at the Cort Theatre, New York

There's a big customer in the show-room, at last —and the firm's models get ready to "hit him right between the eyes."

The moment of triumph—"When you're down, where else can you go but up?"

From the Florodora girls to the *Fifth Season,* From *Ankles Aweigh* to Ziegfeld, Broadway has always understood the attractions of the American woman. [c.1955]

A 44th Street institution since 1921, Sardi's is "the club, mess hall, lounge, post office, saloon and marketplace" for theater people. [c.1955]

Hector's did not represent fine dining, but its cafeteria-style offerings provided the stage for many after-movie feasts. [c.1956]

Lindy's won immortality as "Mindy's" in *Guys and Dolls,* and its cheesecake fueled generations of Times Square visitors from 1921 to 1969. [c.1956]

Times Square in Decline

In the late 1950s, an urban legend developed regarding Times Square: It was an increasingly seedy, disreputable, and sometimes dangerous place to visit. The rumors soon assumed a reality and became indisputable fact. It did not matter that the New York Police Department (NYPD) reported that the Times Square precinct was *not* in the top quarter for reported crime, and indeed had made only four drug arrests in all of 1959. Statistics made no impact on the growing story, and the fifteen "grinder" movies on 42nd Street soon achieved a reputation as dens of vice—havens for prostitutes of both sexes. Inadvertently, Mayor Robert Wagner confirmed the legend in 1961 when he ordered closure of "The Hole," an underground subway passage to the Rialto Theater that had become an infamous "pick-up" location.

As the sexual revolution of the 1960s progressed, Times Square happily joined the movement. Its first 25-cent peepshow opened in 1966, and had multiplied into an estimated 1,000 by 1971. Despite the efforts of five mayors, such establishments continue to exist near Times Square.

An even worse blow to Times Square was the loss of its familiar institutions. The famed Camel smoker puffed his last cigarette in 1966. The Astor Hotel fell to the wrecking ball in 1968, and was replaced by the Minskoff Building (One Astor Place), a less friendly setting that alienated walkers. The classic lines of the *Times* Tower were covered with marble, and became a site for ads encouraging people to read *Newsday.* Even Ripley Believe It or Not Odditorium fled to Los Angeles at the end of 1971. "Times Square used to be the best tourist area of the world," said Ripley's departing manager, "but it's gone downhill severely." In leaving, he called Broadway an "Avenue of Perverts."

New York critics were quick to point out similar 42nd Street declines. The site where Murray's Roman Gardens had once reigned, where Hubert's Flea Circus once entertained, was now a live sex emporium. The Times Square area held almost one hundred such establishments by the late 1970s, and many did not even have glass

By the 1980s, the transformation of 42nd Street into "Sin Street" was a well-documented fact. [c.1985]

Times Square in Decline

partitions between the performers and the clients. Ten thousand disgusted feminists held a public march against pornography at the end of the decade. Not surprisingly, Hollywood found it profitable to join the rising tide of condemnation. The best movie of 1969 was *Midnight Cowboy,* a study of the rough trade of male prostitution in Times Square.

Squalor and sleaze seemed characteristic of the new Times Square. The area around the Port Authority Bus Terminal had never been uplifting, but the presence of many young prostitutes won it infamy as "The Minnesota Strip." The NYPD, by administratively dividing the area into Midtown North and South in 1972, inadvertently confirmed a public perception that crime had doubled. In defiance of statistics and successive "clean-up" orders from City Hall, 42nd Street became "Sin Street," and Times Square was perceived as an urban battlefield. And the ever grimmer statistics that emerged from the "drug wars" of the 1970s only confirmed the impression that the city was losing the battle. Regardless of how many hit shows flourished on the cross streets and despite the glittering signs, the "Great White Way" had become tarnished. Native New Yorkers increasingly shunned the area while tourists came to gaze at its degradation, not its attractions. An urban legend had been created, and evidence on the ground seemed to confirm its reality. For the rest of the century, New York City would struggle to restore the lost luster of Times Square and reclaim it for the public. Only gradually did a coalition of businessmen, politicians, and community groups convince a skeptical audience of natives and visitors that Times Square was not hazardous to their health.

Times Square held over 100 "sex shops" before its revival began in the 1990s. [c.1985]

George M. Cohan offers his "regards to Broadway" in Duffy Square, and might be casting a glance at the world's largest sign above the Victoria Theater. [c.1964]

Several years after the photo on page 149 was taken, the *Times* Tower was clothed in "Miami Beach Marble," while the Astor Hotel awaited the wrecking ball. [c.1966]

Forty-Second Street, the "Street of Dreams" that inspired dozens of movies, had become the most dangerous street in the metropolis by the mid-sixties. [c.1967]

The forbidding mass of the bus terminal, a parking lot on 42nd Street, and porn movies were characteristic of "Sin Street" before Times Square's revival began. [c.1970]